Cry Liberty

D0088515

New Narratives in American History

Series Editors
James West Davidson
Michael B. Stoff

Colonial

Southern

Civil War and Reconstruction

Twentieth-Century Environmental

African American

Twentieth-Century U.S. History

Cry Liberty

THE GREAT STONO RIVER SLAVE
REBELLION OF 1739

PETER CHARLES HOFFER

OXFORD
UNIVERSITY PRESS

OXFORD
UNIVERSITY PRESS

Oxford University Press, Inc., publishes works
that further Oxford University's objective of excellence
in research, scholarship, and education.

Oxford   New York

Auckland   Cape Town   Dar es Salaam   Hong Kong   Karachi
Kuala Lumpur   Madrid   Melbourne   Mexico City   Nairobi
New Delhi   Shanghai   Taipei   Toronto

With offices in

Argentina   Austria   Brazil   Chile   Czech Republic   France   Greece
Guatemala   Hungary   Italy   Japan   Poland   Portugal   Singapore
South Korea   Switzerland   Thailand   Turkey   Ukraine   Vietnam

For titles covered by Section 112 of the US Higher Education
Opportunity Act, please visit www.oup.com/us/he for the
latest information about pricing and alternate formats.

Published by Oxford University Press, Inc.
198 Madison Avenue, New York, New York 10016
www.oup.com

Oxford is a registered trademark of Oxford University Press

Library of Congress Cataloging-in-Publication Data
Hoffer, Peter Charles, 1944–
Cry liberty : the great Stono River slave rebellion of 1739 / Peter Charles Hoffer.
p.   cm. — (New narratives in American history)
Includes bibliographical references and index.
ISBN 978-0-19-538661-5; 978-0-19-538660-8 (pbk.)
1. Slave insurrections—South Carolina—Stono—History—18th century.
2. Stono (S.C.)—Race relations—History—18th century.
3. South Carolina—Race relations—History—18th century.
4. Slavery—South Carolina—History—18th century.   I. Title.
F279.S84H64 2010
975.7'02—dc22   2010000643

7 9 8

Printed in Canada
on acid-free paper

CONTENTS

Contents

Foreword

WHEN HISTORIANS DEBATE THE CONTOURS OF THEIR CRAFT, the concepts of *narrative* and *contingency* are closely linked. The outcome of any series of events depends—is contingent—upon the decisions of individuals. Historical narrative traces the sequence of those decisions; each forking point signifies a split between roads taken and not taken. Understanding the broader context in which such decisions takes place is, of course, essential: the way a society is organized, the relations among classes, the cultural and intellectual landscapes. But narrative insists that individual actions are not merely an inevitable by-product of society's overarching structures. So Peter Hoffer would have us recall when it comes to the literal forks in the road leading to the Stono rebellion of 1739.

Stono was the only full-scale slave rebellion to erupt in the British colonies of North America. Despite its relative magnitude, and despite the first panicked and then ferocious responses of South Carolina's white residents, little information about the outbreak has survived. We catch glimpses of a band of slaves marching down Pon Pon Road, which linked Charleston with

Savannah; we hear drums beating and spy a flag hoisted at the head of the procession. Various reports permit us to make out the charred, smoking houses scattered in the procession's wake. In short, we see clearly a rebellion in progress. But how did the uprising get to that point? What were the contingencies along the way, the long-held grudges or incidental sparks that brought these people together to tramp along the road?

Historians reconstructing the events of September 1739 most often have suggested that where there is fire there must have been much smoke: that is, there must have been a conspiracy devised at least days, perhaps weeks, in advance, and a plan of action laid out among the ringleaders. White planters perennially warned of such plots and were nervously attentive to any rumors of rebellion. Surely several dozen slaves did not find themselves assembled on the king's highway burning houses and beating drums by sheer happenstance.

Peter Hoffer has combed the records in an effort to clear the ground of any unwarranted suppositions of what "surely" must have been. Where the record is so sparse, we likely will never know with certainty what brought these slaves to Pon Pon Road. Yet Hoffer ably suggests a narrative in which contingency is paramount. Perhaps these men did not start out intending to raise slaves in rebellion throughout the countryside. Is it possible that one unexpected event led to another, and then yet another, slowly narrowing options and forcing choices?

Such a reconstruction pushes narrative and contingency to the outermost boundaries of what can be summoned from the past. In doing so, Hoffer's narrative leads us to look at the "evil" at Stono in unexpected ways. The men whose resistance in the end proved heroic may not have been, to begin with, heroes at all. Rather than a desperate conspiracy, the rebellion may have been prodded into being step by small step as "the natural outcome," in Hoffer's words, "of the everyday deformities of slavery." In this volume within the New Narratives in American History series, contingency and narrative walk hand in hand.

James West Davidson
Michael B. Stoff
Series Editors

INTRODUCTION AND ACKNOWLEDGMENTS

❧

The only large-scale slave rebellion in the British North American colonies occurred on a single day, from very early Sunday morning to late afternoon, on September 9, 1739. The setting was similarly limited—a store, a bridge, nearby plantations, and a road along the North Branch of the Stono River, in the Low Country of South Carolina. Compared to the massive slave uprisings in Jamaica, Hispaniola, Dutch Surinam, and other New World colonies, the sixty to one hundred slave rebels and the twenty-three white victims were a small cast of characters. Marching down Pon Pon Road, the slaves "cried liberty" but for those whites who lived through the terror, "every breast was filled with concern.... Evil brought home to us within our very doors awakened the attention of the most unthinking... at such danger."[1]

1. "Report of the Committee Appointed to Enquire into the Causes of the Disappointment of Success in the Late Expedition against St. Augustine," July 1, 1741, *The Colonial Records of South Carolina: Journal of the Commons House of Assembly, May 18, 1741–July 10, 1742*, ed. J. H. Easterby (Columbia: South Carolina Historical Commission, 1953), 84.

Stono was more than a single terrifying event. It remains for historians a vexing puzzle. Despite the black majority in South Carolina (and thousands of enslaved men and women in the other planter colonies), "the lack of prolonged or wide-spread slave rebelliousness," as Philip Morgan put it, was a phenomenon in itself. Why were there no other uprisings? Why did the Stono rebellion differ from the common run of events? Was slavery so repressive in North America and whites so determined and efficient in ferreting out slave conspiracies that rebellion never had a chance—except at Stono? Certainly, whites worried obsessively about slave rebellion, an obsession escalating to "near panic" when evidence pointed to such conspiracies.[2]

Here is the story as we have told it up to now: Slaves newly imported from Africa, warriors in spirit and by training, working on plantations twenty miles from the colonial capital of Charles Town (renamed Charleston after the American Revolution), hearing of the coming war between the English and the Spanish empires, decided to rebel. During the night they broke into a storehouse to obtain guns, killed and burned out the white planters they encountered, and marched to the sound of two drums down a packed earth road toward the Spanish colony of Florida. They tried to enlist the slaves in the neighborhood to join the rebellion. They sought the freedom that the Spanish promised to runaway slaves. Brave, if bloody, their acts mirrored the horrors

2. Philip Morgan, *Slave Counterpoint: Black Culture in the Eighteenth-Century Chesapeake and Low Country* (Chapel Hill: University of North Carolina Press, 1998), 386; Peter Charles Hoffer, *The Great New York Conspiracy of 1741: Slavery, Crime, and Colonial Law* (Lawrence: University Press of Kansas, 2003), 73.

of slavery itself, and the violence they offered to the masters matched the violence that slavery inflicted on its black victims. They died in battle.[3]

But have we told the only story we might tell? The rebellion may not have begun that way at all. There is a curious backward flow of events to the conventional account. If there were Angolan soldiers leading the band in the morning, there must have been Angolan soldiers leading the mayhem the night before; if the plan in the morning was to raise rebellion, there must have been a plan in place the evening before to raise rebellion; if all who marched down the road in the morning had committed themselves to rebellion, then all who took some part in the night's activities must have had the same solemn motivation as the rebels. This is the logical fallacy of post hoc ergo propter hoc—if later, then before. It turns causation around, making later events into the cause of earlier ones.

If we have told the story backward, imputing rebellion to those who had, at first, very different intentions, are we missing a more important lesson in the entire episode than the one we find in our textbooks? If the story's beginning is neither so dramatic nor so heroic, for that very reason we need to understand more clearly the parts that circumstance and chance played in the lives of enslaved men and masters alike.

3. The capsule story that appears, for example, in Ira Berlin, *Many Thousands Gone: The First Two Centuries of Slavery in North America* (Cambridge, Mass.: Harvard University Press, 1998), 73; and Robert Olwell, *Masters, Slaves, and Subjects: The Culture of Power in the South Carolina Low Country, 1740–1790* (Baltimore: Johns Hopkins University Press, 1998), 21.

I have been living with the Stono story for nearly two decades. I wrestled with it in the course of writing a textbook on early American history, revisited it in a book about the senses and history, and began to doubt the story that I, and everyone else, was telling when I tried to recount what had happened in a New York City slave rebellion two years after Stono. I believed then, and still would like to believe, that everyone who resisted slavery, whatever their status or ancestry, was a hero. Whatever means they used was justified by the horror of the institution itself. But did this mean that resistance always began as resistance, or that overturning slavery was the immediate aim in every act of resistance? Was rebellion always the aim of those who raised their hands against oppression and ventured their lives against the system that bound them? This book is not an answer to that question, for it concerns only one episode of resistance. Even so, I know my reading of the sources and my conclusions may not be acceptable to everyone. Indeed, some of what I found greatly disturbed me. But stories like Stono do not always reveal the heroes and villains we would like to find; rather, slavery demeaned and brutalized everyone it touched.[4]

As I wrestled with these questions, I lamented the fact that there was so little in the historical record directly on the uprising. Why had such a major event—the first mass slave uprising in the British continental colonies, an event that con-

4. Peter Charles Hoffer, *The Brave New World: A History of Early America*, 1st ed. (Boston: Houghton Mifflin, 2001); 341–342; Hoffer, *Sensory Worlds in Early America* (Baltimore: Johns Hopkins University Press, 2003) 137–149; Hoffer, *Great New York Conspiracy*, passim.

tinued to live in the nightmares of whites and the daydreams of blacks for more than a hundred years—left so little record? Where were the eyewitness accounts? The interrogation of those suspected of aiding and abetting the rebellion? Surely a government like South Carolina's, which recorded every shipment of slaves entering the port of Charles Town, would have thoroughly documented this momentous episode.

Was an official silence imposed? The *South-Carolina Gazette* published nothing about the uprising. News of the uprising spread in British periodicals such as *Gentleman's Magazine and London Magazine* and colonial newspapers such as the *Boston Evening-Post*, but not a word appeared locally until the legislature returned to its deliberations that fall. Alarming reports of slave uprisings might deter white migrants and, equally important, investment in the Low Country economy. While some uprisings were widely publicized, information about others was suppressed. After masters and militia coerced evidence, using torture, of an alleged plot among slaves in the Mississippi Delta in the first months of the Confederacy, according to the historian Winthrop Jordan, "no official accounting was ever made. In Adams County [Mississippi] . . . 'vigilance' committees kept things as quiet as possible." The semiofficial veil of silence to which masters acceded could not stop slaves from whispering about the secret executions, or whites from writing to relatives, but it was only the survival of a fragmentary verbatim account of the examination of slaves that allowed Jordan to envision the tumult and penetrate the silences at Second Creek. As Mark Smith has written about slave resistance in the nineteenth century, "Masters wisely and readily kept their mouths shut and accepted their own enforced silence as the price for perpetuating human bondage and their own authority."[5]

Slaves also knew the value of silence. Whether slaves fled in silence, or malingered in silence, or simply left the quarters at night in silence, it was silence that created space and time for slaves away from their bondage. Muted talk, gesture, and glance were part of all conspiracies, from those formed to steal eggs to those arranged to run away. Silence was a weapon when called and refusing to come, or when verbally or physically abused.[6]

To penetrate these silences is my goal and my challenge here.

Acknowledgments

For research and writing assistance rendered, support for the project, and good fellowship, I am grateful to Charles Lesser, South Carolina Department of Archives and History (SCDAH); Martha Zierden, Charleston Museum; and J. Tracy Power of the SCDAH. Marjoline Kars, Justin Pope, and Jason Sharples shared their research. Fellow UGA folks Alex Massengale, Hayden Smith, and Michael Winship; along with Sylvia Frey, S. Max Edelson, Philip Morgan, Robert Olwell, and Robert Paquette read the

5. David A. Copeland, *Colonial American Newspapers: Character and Content* (Newark: University of Delaware Press, 1997), 139–140, 147; Winthrop D. Jordan, *Tumult and Silence at Second Creek: An Inquiry into a Civil War Slave Conspiracy, rev. ed.* (Baton Rouge: Louisiana State University Press, 1995), 5–6; Mark M. Smith, *Listening to Nineteenth-Century America* (Chapel Hill: University of North Carolina Press, 2001), 72.

6. Smith, *Listening to Nineteenth-Century America*, 67–68.

manuscript and commented. James West Davidson, a co-editor of Oxford University Press's New Narratives in American History series, not only encouraged the project from the outset and guided it through the acceptance process at OUP but read and re-read, edited, and did so much more. Brian Wheel, an acquisitions editor at OUP, facilitated the approval of the proposal and guided the manuscript through publication. Calvin Schermerhorn, Douglas Egerton, Vincent Mikkelsen, and two other anonymous readers for OUP were immensely helpful. The Johns Hopkins University Press and the University Press of Kansas allowed me to recast portions of accounts I had published with them. Thanks to editors and friends Robert Brugger and Michael Briggs for that courtesy.

To all the folks who stopped what they were doing and chatted with an interloper in the Low Country, I dedicate this book. It is their history I tried to tell, and I am grateful for the trust they reposed in me to tell it.

Cry Liberty

· Prologue ·

THE LAND AND THE WATER

❦

In 1722 a remarkable character arrived in Charles Town, South Carolina. The forty-year-old English gentleman scientist Mark Catesby was a collector of botanical specimens, naturalist, artist, and travel writer. The Americas, particularly the West Indies and the Southern colonies, fascinated him. With letters of introduction in hand from the former lieutenant governor of South Carolina, Francis Nicholson, Catesby visited with the rice nabobs—the great planters—and the mercantile agents, and toured the countryside. For two years he took notes and drew minutely detailed pictures of plants from all over the Low Country and the backwoods of the colony.

In his *Natural History of Florida, Carolina, and the Bahamas* (1731), Catesby described what he saw and heard. The climate in summer was "sultry," but in early fall the nights cooled. Rain filled these autumn days "in great quantities...overflowing all the savannah and lower ground." Sometimes fierce lighting strikes split trees and shook the land itself. "Violent storms" brought roaring tides and winds ashore, and "some low situated houses not far from the sea were undermined and carried away

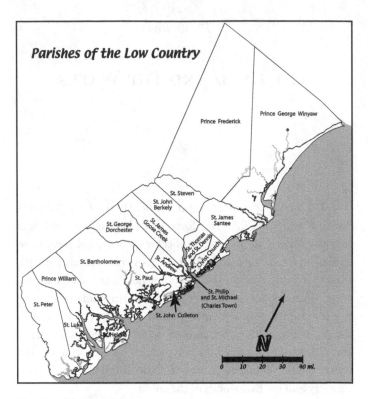

Parishes of the Low Country.

with the inhabitants." These were the "hurracans" that lashed the coastline with hundred-mile-an-hour winds and soaked the land with torrents of rain. The Low Country averaged nine to ten feet above sea level (some of the barrier islands were no more than three- to four-foot-high sand dunes) and the storm surge (waves and high tide) could carry ships moored along the shore as far as three miles inland. But the land was good and worth the trouble of cultivation. The many water passages through the islands were natural highways, and in winter there were no killing frosts.[1]

Another gentleman traveler, some twelve years later, offered an endorsement of creature comforts in the colony. The plantations he saw "were beautiful," he thought, many with substantial brick walls, and the pine forests were wholesome, though the rivers "were very liable to overflow, and the freshets being then so very high" that he and his traveling companion were forced to find a ferry crossing miles away from their intended path.[2]

For some, South Carolina seemed a veritable Eden. As Thomas Bee recalled, "The inhabitants remarkable for the politeness and hospitality and being generally in easy and affluent circumstances, enable them to live in a style of grandeur." One South Carolinian even waxed poetic in his praise of the land:

> Magnolias bright with glossy leaves and flowers,
> Fragrant as Eden in its happiest hours;
> The gloomy cypress, towering to the skies,
> The maple, loveliest in autumnal dyes,
> The palm armorial, with its tufted head,

1. Amy R. W. Meyers and Margaret Beck Pritchard, *Empire's Nature: Mark Catesby's New World Vision* (Chapel Hill: University of North Carolina Press, 1996), 7–8; Mark Catesby, *Natural History* [1731] in *The Colonial South Carolina Scene: Contemporary Views, 1697–1774*, ed. H. Roy Merrens (Columbia: University of South Carolina Press, 1977), 91–93.
2. "A Gentleman's Travels," in Merrens, *Colonial South Carolina*, 113.

Vines over all in wild luxuriance spread,
And columned pines, a mystic wood, he sees,
That sigh and whisper to the passing breeze.[3]

Indeed, the Low Country was a garden of Eden...after the Fall. Although everything grew in abundance, people faced suffering and sudden death day in and day out. The swamp and the savannah were alive with insects, by day biting flies and gnats, by night swarming, bloodsucking mosquitoes. Worse than the pain and itch of bites was the fact that the insects were vectors of deadly disease. Human and animal waste sitting in the stagnant estuaries of the rivers incubated "fluxes and cholera morbus...either acute or chronic," and all manner of fevers. Some fevers repeated, coming and going with the warm weather or the cold. Contemporaries blamed vapors, the heat itself, and the water, "corrupted and stagnated." Smallpox was the worst of the plagues. It came with the ships and struck Charles Town without warning. One worried observer remarked in 1760 that "the people in Charles Town were inoculation mad...and rushed into it with...precipitation," but the pox still carried off hundreds.[4]

The year 1738 was especially pestiferous. Nearly 650 whites were afflicted with the smallpox, 157 of whom died. More than

3. Thomas Bee, "Answers to the Several Questions..." [1781–1783] in Alexander Moore, "Thomas Bee's Notes on the State of Virginia," *Journal of the Early Republic* 7 (Summer 1987), 119; William Grayson, *Hireling and the Slave...and Other Poems* (Charleston, S.C.: McCarter, 1856), 30.

4. James Glen, *A Description of South Carolina* (London: Dodsley, 1751), 44–45; Eliza Lucas Pinckney to Mrs. Evance, March 15, 1760, *The Letterbook of Eliza Lucas Pinckney, 1739–1762*, ed. Elise Pinckney (Chapel Hill: University of North Carolina Press, 1972), 148.

one thousand blacks suffered from the pox, and 138 were recorded to have died from it. A third of Charles Town was sick. Many more in the city would die of the "malignant" or yellow fever. The next year was little better. At the end of August, the Charles Town merchant Robert Pringle wrote to his Boston counterpart John Erving, "It is likewise very sickly here at present both in town and country, a great many people being affected with…fevers and agues." Lieutenant Governor William Bull prorogued the assembly, deciding that the summer session would take place in November, due to the "sickness."[5]

Early modern cities like Charles Town were especially prey to diseases sustained by poor sanitation, such as dysentery (the "bloody flux"), typhus, and typhoid fever. Hot and humid climates fostered the even more fatal yellow fever's carriers, mosquitoes. Worst of all was the "quotidian ague" or malaria, a parasitical infestation brought to the American coasts from Africa. So widespread and uncontrollable was this disease that the Carolinians became expert in describing its symptoms, although no one knew how to avoid it. Pringle was still in town, but many had fled, seeking safety in the country: "Death was everywhere."[6]

---

5. *Boston Gazette*, November 13–20, 1738; *South-Carolina Gazette*, November 5, 1738; John Duffy, "Yellow Fever in Colonial Charleston," *South Carolina Historical and Genealogical Magazine* 52 (1951), 194; Robert Pringle to John Erving, August 29, 1739, in *The Letterbook of Robert Pringle*, ed. Walter B. Edgar (Columbia, S.C.: University of South Carolina Press, 1972), 1:132; *South Carolina Gazette*, September 8–15, 1739, p. 1.

6. Peter A. Coclanis, *The Shadow of a Dream: Economic Life and Death in the South Carolina Low Country, 1670–1920* (New York: Oxford University Press, 1989), 41–42; Peter Wood, *Black Majority: Negroes in Colonial South Carolina through the Stono Rebellion* (New York: Norton, 1973), 72–73.

European diseases had reduced once-populous Indian communities to ghost towns. Their numbers had shrunk because they had no inherited immunity to the measles, mumps, chickenpox, smallpox, and other diseases the Europeans brought. Faced also with "trade abuses, envy, mounting debts that could not be repaid, and fear of enslavement," and racked by wars among themselves and with the English, most of the surviving Indians moved inland. A few Indian men still fished the rivers and traversed the swampy creek and river courses hunting for game or hired themselves out as boatmen, messengers, or pursuers of runaway slaves. A few Indian women sold their wares at market.

The native peoples left behind them a landscape profoundly transformed. The Indians' burning of coastal brush and trees created savannahs, grassy flat lands fringed by salt marsh. Though thicket covered the gardens the Indians had carved in the midst of cypress and oak forests, the soil of these parklike landscapes was perfect for colonial agriculture. Inadvertently, the Indians had prepared the way for European cultivators.[7]

By the time Catesby toured the Low Country, English-style farmhouses and African-inspired slave quarters dotted the

7. Alfred W. Crosby, *The Columbian Exchange: Biological and Cultural Consequences of 1492* (New York: Praeger, 2003), 42–43; Alan Gallay, *The Indian Slave Trade: The Rise of the English Empire in the American South, 1670–1717* (New Haven, Conn.: Yale University Press, 2003), 330, 338; David Duncan Wallace, *The History of South Carolina* (New York: New York Historical Society, 1934), 1:366; Peter H. Wood, "The Changing Population of the Colonial South, An Overview by Race and Region," in *Powhatan's Mantle: Indians in the Colonial Southeast*, ed. Peter H. Wood, Gregory A. Waselkov, and Thomas Hatley (Lincoln: University of Nebraska Press, 1989), 46–56.

Low Country marsh grasses (photograph by author).

landscape. Once-extensive stands of oak and cypress receded before the newcomers' axes and saws. At the edges of the newly cleared fields, brackish tidal marshes remained. Their grasses provided superb fodder for the Englishmen's cattle.[8]

Slow-moving, shallow rivers and creeks framed these coastal lands. Some of the waterways were natural canals, shifting in their courses after the great storms, dividing the Low Country

8. Robert Weir, *Colonial South Carolina, A History* (Millwood, N.Y.: KTO, 1983), 37–38; Timothy Silver, *A New Face on the Countryside: Indians, Colonists, and Slaves in the South Atlantic Forests, 1500–1800* (New York: Cambridge University Press, 1990), 174; S. Max Edelson, "Clearing Swamps, Harvesting Forests: Trees and the Making of a Plantation Landscape in the Colonial South Carolina Lowcountry," *Agricultural History* 81 (Summer 2007), 381–406.

into smaller and smaller segments. The first of the rivers that any traveler brushed against on his way south and west from Charles Town was the Stono. It is a tidal river that overflowed its banks when the freshets came, black at night, green in the day. The river course is a lazy question mark emptying into the Atlantic ten miles south of the Charles Town peninsula.

Driven by wind and ocean tide, the body of the Stono undulated through swampy lowlands until it was two miles from the city, then, as if offended by the sight of so many people, it curled to the west. A bridge spanned the Stono where the Main Road connected Kings Highway with Johns Island. Ten miles downstream, the Stono swerved south, its banks narrowing and its

The Stono River (photograph by author).

slow-moving waters draining into the Wadmalaw River. More a channel or an estuary than a river course, the Stono was the Low Country in miniature.

The Stono and its continuation, the Wadmalaw River, along with the North Edisto (really a branch of the South Edisto jutting into Wadmalaw Sound), cut off three islands from the mainland—Johns Island, Wadmalaw Island, and Kiawah Island. The Wadmalaw and the North Edisto are the eastern boundary of Edisto Island, and all four islands were part of St. Pauls' Parish.

In 1733 the South Carolina legislature, a body of freeholders elected by the parishes of the various counties, decided that the three islands within the bends of the Stono should form one electoral district, the parish of St. Johns, Colleton County. They carved St. Johns out of the older parish of St. Paul's.

The parish was the local unit of administrative activity and responsibility. All courts were located in the capital, but commissioners, men of property and standing in the parish, were named to manage the patrols at night, clear the riverways, oversee the drainage of swamps, and cut and maintain the roads. Often the men chosen refused the work, even though they were paid for it. Refusal brought fines, but this did not instill greater public spirit.[9]

On these islands there are no natural landmarks. As though the nearby ocean had inspired the landscape, it rose and fell in

9. "An Act for Dividing the Parish of St. Paul's in Colleton County," 1733, *The First Published Laws of South Carolina*, ed. John D. Cushman (Wilmington, Del.: Glazier, 1982), 138.

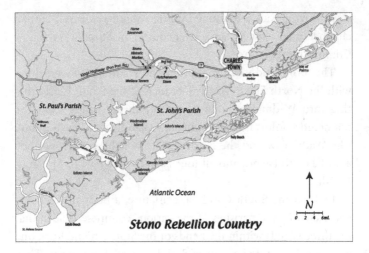

Stono rebellion country.

gentle waves, its highest mounds no more than twenty-five feet above sea level. Creeks ran a crooked course into the river, and marshy lowland, labeled swamps in the eighteenth century and now recognized as essential wetlands, made passage along the fields treacherous. Today, some roads still dead-end into marsh or reclaimed farmland.

How hard it must have been in 1739 to find one's way from dwelling to dwelling. There were no signposts, as there were in New England or the home country. In 1726 the inhabitants of the island, "by their petition to the general assembly," explained that they were "situated remote from any established road" and that the land had "deep and almost impassible swamps," thereby preventing people from reaching any house of worship, much less Charles Town.[10]

Plantation owners and yeomen farmers had to be hospitable to white visitors. They would not only help newcomers get around but would even put up a stranger for a meal or the night and lend a slave to lead the traveler down the road or through the fields in the direction of the traveler's destination. The fields themselves were open. Wood was still plentiful for heating and building and fencing (although fencing-in land was a touchy issue among the planters). Hogs were allowed to range openly. Cattle and horses were penned, their value so great that the expense of fencing them in was reluctantly borne.

In the first half of the eighteenth century, St. Johns' Parish filled with adventurous immigrants. The Gibbs family had arrived shortly after the turn of the century and owned more than a thousand acres. John Fenwick alighted in 1721, and soon his plantation was a going concern. The Moores owned as much land as the Gibbses, but not as much as Hugh Hext and his son Alexander. The rest of the coastal lands were divided into much smaller parcels among three dozen grantees. Many came and went. More than a few died. Some of those who survived prospered, for rice, their stock in trade, was lucrative. The Stanyarnes, the Hexts, the Joneses, and their kin (for all the planters intermarried) became families of means and status. They built their two-story brick-and-frame homes on bluffs overlooking the river, hoping to use the tidal reaches to manage

10. "An Act for Making a New Road between the North and the Middle Branch of the Stono River," 1726, *The Earliest Printed Laws of South Carolina, 1692–1734*, ed. John D. Cushing (Wilmington, Del.: Glazier, 1982), 464.

the rice crop. But storm tides and rising waters made cultivation chancy, as chancy as life and death in the Low Country.[11]

❧

Today, all of old Colleton is now part of Charleston County, and the landscape is changing again. Some of the old rice fields are now part of elegantly gated subdivisions, golf courses, mini-malls, and retirement-housing estates, such as the ironically named "Hope Plantation." Other portions of the once-sprawling plantation lands are now second-growth forests. The widest part of the river, opposite James Island, looks out at marinas and condo estates, beyond which lies Charleston itself. It is part of the U.S. Intercoastal Waterway. Up the river, paralleling U.S. 17, the salt-water marsh grasses fill the landscape. The green water, shallow and tidal, suggests an earlier, less hurried time.

U.S. 17 is a four-lane divided highway whose traffic—SUVs and semis—flies by at sixty miles an hour. Off the major artery, on back roads such as Old Jacksonborough Road and Parker's Ferry Road, traffic is far sparser. Along these roads the slave rebels marched and the militia rode. Today, a few nineteenth-century plantation homes lie untouched, abandoned when rice cultivation ended in the 1920s. The estate developers have not reached these Low Country byways yet. Portions of the roads are unpaved. Over them arch moss-laded hardwoods, much as they would have in slavery times. On one, a recent traveler saw barefoot prints in the packed earth.

11. Laylon Wayne Jordan and Elizabeth H. Stringfellow, *A Place Called St. John's: The Story of John's, Edisto, Wadmalaw, Kiawah, and Seabrook Islands of South Carolina* (Spartanburg, S.C.: The Reprint Company, 1998), 56–75, 234–235, 237.

Traveling these back roads on a muggy late-summer afternoon in 2008, even a visitor used to Georgia summers finds the heat oppressive. The humidity clings. No-see-ums are not repelled by the most liberal dose of DEET. At dusk, the road grows quiet, and the farther one travels along it, the farther one seems to penetrate into the past. From four lanes to two lanes, from lighted subdivisions to dark and brooding old fields dimly visible beyond the headlights, each mile takes a visitor another decade or two into the past.

Where the Wallace River (a tributary of the Stono once named Wallace Creek), meets U.S. 17, a historical marker stands. Its placement is based somewhat on conjecture for the South Carolina Department of Archives and History did not know exactly where it belonged when they set it at the edge of the road, in 2006. As the historian and archivist J. Tracy Power recalled,

> The Stono Rebellion marker was erected in 2006 by the Sea Island Farmers Cooperative in Rantowles, not far from the site of a store on Wallace Creek where the rebellion began. I worked with Mr. Curtis Inabinett, Sr., of the Sea Island Farmers Cooperative—also a former state legislator—on the text for the marker, and also consulted with archaeologists Martha Zierden and Ron Anthony, public historian Shawn Halifax, and Mark Smith of the University of South Carolina on the text. Mr. Inabinett and the Sea Island Farmers Cooperative originally wanted the marker to be specific (in terms of yards, or even feet), saying that the rebellion began "here," but I was unwilling, based on the evidence, to say more than "nearby." As you will see from the text below, we finally arrived at "nearby," which I believe is accurate.[12]

12. J. Tracy Power to the author, email, October 29, 2008. I am grateful to Dr. Power for this inside information. "The marker was placed at the Sea Island Farmers Cooperative for better visibility on U.S. Highway 17, something our marker program did more often in the early days of

The marker itself reads: "The Stono Rebellion (1739). The Stono Rebellion, the largest Slave insurrection in North America, began nearby on September 9, 1739. About twenty Africans raided a store near Wallace Creek, a branch of the Stono River. Taking guns and other weapons they killed two shopkeepers. The rebels marched south toward promised freedom in Spanish Florida, waving flags, beating drums, and shouting 'liberty.'" The marker does not reveal what happened to the proud band of slave rebels, and in fact much of the story the marker tells is disputable. But something did happen nearby, and that event changed history.[13]

---

the program (from the 1930s to the 1950s) than recently. I'd prefer placing markers directly at the site being marked, but of course in this case it would be virtually impossible to pinpoint a precise location. I do think the site eventually chosen, and the final text, are appropriate."

13. I traveled to the marker on September 12, 2008, and waited there as night fell. Cars whizzed by. The heat very slowly dissipated. A torrential rainstorm flooded the road. When the rain had passed, the humidity remained. The language on the marker seems to me to track that in Walter D. Edgar's *History of South Carolina* (Columbia: University of South Carolina Press, 1998), 74–75. Edgar, a longtime professor of history at the Columbia campus of the University of South Carolina, is a widely acknowledged expert in the state's history.

When the marker was erected, the Charleston newspaper reported that the sign commemorated an "unsuccessful" rebellion. John Shuler ("Calling Out Liberty: Human Rights Discourse and Early American Literature," PhD diss., City University of New York, 2007, p. 227), disagrees: "There is evidence that this claim that the rebellion was unsuccessful is false. The fact of the persistence of the story—a narrative of action, of boldness, of engagement by an abused people—is indicative of its success." While I respect the moral imperative in this assertion, logically it means that any event remembered by scholars, "how we make sense of our world" through the stories we tell, can be turned into a success retroactively. The rebellion was not a success in any sense of the word then, and we cannot change history to suit ourselves.

· *One* ·

AT HUTCHENSON'S STORE

❧

THE CAROLINA COLONY CAME INTO EXISTENCE WITH A LEGAL document. In 1663 Charles II of England granted the Carolinas to eight of the men who enabled him to return to England from his exile in France after the English interregnum. The colony was a "proprietorship" or private holding of these men, who saw it as an opportunity for personal gain. The southern portion of the grant, later called South Carolina, beckoned the planters of the West Indies. They needed to feed the slaves who worked on their sugar plantations in the Caribbean. Peter Colleton, son of one of the eight proprietors, Sir John Colleton, owned land and slaves in Barbados, and pioneered the immigration. In 1670 the first boatload arrived—planters, servants, and a handful of Barbadian slaves. For three decades the incoming settlers looked for a profitable staple crop, herded their livestock, and imported slaves. With the expansion of rice cultivation came the profits that the proprietors had envisioned. Politically, the proprietorship was a failure, and the North and South Carolina colonies became royal provinces in 1719. But economically, South Carolina prospered. By 1729 the

Carolina rice lands extended from the coast many miles inland, the proprietors' descendants had surrendered their charter to the crown, and slaves were a majority of the colony's population.[1]

Standing on a low bluff above the Stono River next to the Main Road bridge connecting the Kings Highway to Johns Island on a muggy summer day in 1739, one could hardly have known how prosperous the colony was. The only structure in sight was Hutchenson's store, a single-story, clapboard emporium looking more like a barn than anything else. The story of the Stono uprising began here. So did my journey through the Low Country. The precise location of the store, still no more than educated conjecture on my part, may not be as important as its function. For where the rude wooden building stood, there came together European, African, and American worlds. Those worlds were tied together by the movement of people, goods, and ideas across distant oceans to the Carolina coast and upriver.[2]

1. David Duncan Wallace, *The History of South Carolina* (New York: New-York Historical Society, 1934), 1:74; Peter Wood, *Black Majority: Negroes in Colonial South Carolina through the Stono Rebellion* (New York: Norton, 1973), 14, 20–21.

2. Historians are still not sure of the store's precise location. Robert Weir (*Colonial South Carolina, A History* [Millwood, N.Y.: KTO, 1983], 193) puts it fifteen miles from Charleston. Wood (*Black Majority*, 314) has the store "within twenty miles" of the capital city. Both agree that the North Branch of the Stono was the site, near a ford, a ferry, or a bridge. Robert Olwell (*Masters, Slaves, and Subjects: The Culture of Power in the South Carolina Low Country, 1740–1790* [Baltimore: Johns Hopkins University Press, 1998], 21) is more certain that the revolt took place "twenty miles west" of Charleston, again on the Stono. Laylon Wayne Jordan and Elizabeth H. Stringfellow (*A Place Called St. John's, Edisto, Wadmalaw, Kiawah, and Seabrook Islands of South Carolina* [Spartanburg, S.C.: The Reprint Company, 1998], 80) move the site to St. Pauls' Parish, "on the

The people were laborers and labor managers, immigrants, servants, and slaves. More than three million of these travelers

---

western branch of the Stono River, perhaps ten miles distant from Wadmalaw Island." Ira Berlin (*Many Thousands Gone: The First Two Centuries of Slavery in North America* [Cambridge, Mass.: Harvard University Press, 1998], 73) puts the site of the battle in the field some fifty miles from Florida, meaning that the store must have been closer to the South Edisto River. Mark Smith does not describe the location of the store but has it on the Stono River and reports the slaves marching south from it (Smith, ed., *Stono: Documenting and Interpreting a Southern Slave Revolt* [Columbia: University of South Carolina Press, 2005], xii). Pon Pon Road–U.S. Route 17, then Jacksonborough Road, does not, however, lead south from the river but instead southwest.

The conventional wisdom is that the store was somewhere near or on Wallace Creek, where the creek empties into the Stono. That, at least, is where the South Carolina historical marker puts it; the Stono Insurrection entry in Walter Edgar's *Encyclopedia of South Carolina* and Smith agree (Smith, "Introduction," *Stono*, xv n2).

But there is a more likely site. In 1739 Main Road connected the mainland with Johns Island. The records mention a bridge over the Stono there. One can still see pieces of tabby (lime and seashell) that might have been the foundations of the bridge. Today Main Road still runs from U.S. 17 to Johns Island, but now the bridge is a lovely concrete arch high above the water. The Stono River there is part of the Intercoastal Waterway. At the Johns Island side of the road, underneath the bridge, is a boat slip and a parking lot on a bluff. That is where I would put a store, and where I believe Hutchenson put his.

One might assume that it does not matter precisely where the store was, how far from Charleston, in which parish, St. Johns or St. Pauls, old Colleton County, any more than it matters how many slaves were involved. But what an event is surely does depend upon where it begins. "Where" is a very human part of "what." See, for example, the historian Timothy Breen's search for the Mulford warehouse, a mart similar to Hutchenson's, on the Northwest Harbor coast of East Hampton, Long Island. The site of the warehouse revealed how the people of East Hampton connected themselves the Atlantic world (Breen, *Imagining the Past: East Hampton Histories* [Athens: University of Georgia Press, 1996]).

crossed the Atlantic during the colonial era. There was always a shortage of labor in the Americas, and European colonists were fierce exploiters of labor, their own and others, in the search for wealth. The goods were the staples the colonies produced for the world market, the demand for which drove the colonists from coastal settlement to settlement, and from the coast inland. Food crops and livestock predominated: sugar, tobacco, rice, corn, wheat, cattle, hogs, and horses. The driving force was plantation capitalism producing staple crops that would sate world markets.

Hutchenson's was described by contemporaries as a "warehouse," a "store," and a "plantation." Colonial backwater stores were rarely imposing structures, nothing resembling the brick-walked and elegantly porticoed mansions of great planters. Indeed, the stores looked more like barns than commercial establishments. But the lots or plots of land could accommodate structures of a thousand square feet and more. Most likely of milled or plank-wood construction and planked flooring, Hutchenson's may have boasted a few hand-blown glass windows, with wooden shutters. Within, the space was probably divided by a counter, with rooms off the central display area for storage and keeping accounts. One backwoods Virginia store in 1728 displayed its wares in "casks, chests, crates, barrels, trunks, and boxes." Hutchenson's surely had its share of these.[3]

---

3. Richard Bushman, *The Refinement of America: Persons, Houses, Cities* (New York: Knopf, 1992), 110–113, 124; Martha Zierden, Suzanne Linder, and Ronald Anthony, *Willtown: An Archeological and Historical Perspective* (Charleston, S.C.: Charleston Museum, 1999), 143–159; Ann Smart Martin, *Buying into the World of Goods: Early Consumers in Backcountry Virginia* (Baltimore: Johns Hopkins University Press, 2008), 147–148.

At Hutchenson's, the Atlantic world, linking the rice plantations of the English colony of South Carolina with the merchants of Bristol, Plymouth, and Liverpool, displayed its goods. The wares on the shelves of Hutchenson's store bore witness to how closely the Low Country was tied into the goods and human services network of this Atlantic world. Without capital from England and Scotland, without labor from Europe, Africa, and the Americas, without markets for colonial goods across the ocean, South Carolina would not have been a profitable enterprise.[4]

The settlers were avid consumers of imported goods. By 1739 the entire English-speaking world had succumbed to an obsession with consumer goods and credit buying. The Atlantic world had become a giant mart to supply these "baubles of empire" to colonial buyers. Elites in the home country and its colonies had discovered the pleasures of store-bought goods, and stores imported huge quantities of alcoholic beverages, fancy clothes, chairs with cushions and porcelain dishes to satisfy their customers. As far from Charles Town as Hutchenson's might be, buying and displaying consumer goods was still a passion for the neighborhood's settlers.[5]

Stores like Hutchenson's dotted the coastline of British North America. Wherever ships could put in and offload at the stores' waterside jetties, wherever the hogheads of tobacco, the barrels of whale oil, the sacks of grain and barrels of rice could be hauled onto or ferried out to the vessels, there stood miniature malls. At the Colonial

---

4. Wood, "Colony of a Colony," in *Black Majority*, 13–34.
5. T. H. Breen, *The Marketplace of Revolution: How Consumer Politics Shaped American Independence* (New York: Oxford University Press, 2004), 61–62.

The store site at Colonial Dorchester (photograph by author).

Dorchester historic site on the Ashley River about twenty miles north of Hutchenson's, the ruins of one of these jetties along the waterline remains. Richard Baker's jetty was a structure of notched logs, the spaces within filled with dirt and rubble. At Dorchester, a merchant advertising "the sale of a lot facing the market in 1747" took special care to note that the site, with its house and stores, would be "convenient for a Store-Keeper." Eight years later William Power advertised his intention to open a store and tavern on Dorchester green.[6]

6. Breen, *Imagining the Past*, 144. I visited the colonial Dorchester site on September 2, 2008. The footprint of the wharf was still visible at the edge of the Ashley River. For text, see www.teachingushistory.org/qt-dor/dorchester-transcript.htm.

We will never know what Hutchenson's actually stocked, but William Welsh's store at Willtown, on the South Edisto, displayed tools, clothing, "ivory fans," and "scarlet waistcoats." The inventory of the storekeeper Abraham Schellinger, of East Hampton, Long Island, listed a ready supply of dyes, pewter table- and cooking-ware, and bolts of silk. A backwoods Virginia store included everything from "nails to novels."[7]

Every colonial store kept up a stock of the basics that American customers demanded. In addition, fashion had come to Charles Town, with its newspaper advertising the latest imports from Britain, along with the new fad of shopping. Even a country store like Hutchenson's shelves and counters stocked consumer durables and food, tools, and fabrics, called dry goods. Shoes and candles, writing paper and inks, containers of tobacco and pipes, necessities and "notions" lay next to one another.[8]

Hutchenson's was not an apothecary (the forerunner of the pharmacy), but it surely had some selection of herbal medicines, liquid potions, and medical implements. The better-stocked colonial apothecaries of the time also sold spices, sugar, and molasses candies; salts for the table and the tub; perfumes; spot and stain removers; pills and elixirs for common ailments and pains; "cordials" of various kinds to return the body to vim and vigor; and perhaps specialty items such as "Blackrie's Lixivium for the

---

7. Zierden, Linder, and Anthony, *Willtown*, 56; Breen, *Imagining the Past*, 152; Martin, *Buying into the World of Goods*, 17.

8. Breen, *Marketplace of Revolution*, 124; Shane White and Graham White, *Stylin': African American Expressive Culture from its Beginnings to the Zoot Suit* (Ithaca, N.Y.: Cornell University Press, 1998), 15–16.

Stone and Gravel." Householders doubled as doctors and nurses, masters practiced medicine on their slaves, and notions, potions, and plasters were necessities. Thus, a well-stocked home had to have "syringes, lancets, crucibles, pill boxes, vials," and other instruments.[9]

Planters and farmers needed the tools of their trade, and Hutchenson's must have stocked seeds and gardening tools, hoes, and hand shovels, in addition to an array of hardware. The store offered carpenters tools such as planes, saws, hammers, axes, awls, and adzes, and nails of various sizes; hinges and locks for doors; whitewash and paint; and glass for windows. Farmers doubled as builders and repairers, painters and woodworkers. In the back of the store stood heavier items for the farm animals, such as harnesses, saddles, and plows. This economy ran on human and animal power.

Low Country diets were supplemented with fish and game. On a rack behind the counter at Hutchenson's, if it resembled other country stores, stood muskets, lead shot, and powder, nets, hooks, and rods. Slaves brought game and fish to the store along with the produce of their little gardens. Food preparation and preservation was the work of women, but in the heat of the summer, little could be preserved except by salting or smoking. Everything else had to be consumed fresh. No inventory would be complete without the jugs of rum and bottles of porter, ale, beer, hard cider, and wine—and a few glasses for the thirsty to sample the wares. The water was never

9. The list is from the Pasteur and Galt apothecary shop in colonial Williamsburg. See www.history.org/Almanack/places/hb/hbpast.cfm.

as safe to drink as distilled spirits, nor so refreshing to colonial palates.[10]

Hutchenson's was also a staples warehouse—an intermediate stop for rice being moved from the newly planted inland fields to the great wharves in Charles Town. Carolina planters grew rice in the 1690s, but it did not become the colony's major crop until the 1720s. The arrival from Africa of a new variety of rice seed, joined with the skills of blacks from parts of Africa familiar with rice cultivation, turned what had seemed at first an unprofitable experiment (alongside silk, wine, and orange groves) into a goldmine. The key to rice cultivation was a sufficiently large year-round labor force on the plantation. Governor James Glen reported that planters needed about thirty slaves in the field to ensure the profitability of their rice lands.[11]

A joint project of slave and planter, a system of artificial irrigation sluices and gates enabled planters to move inland from the coast. As the historian S. Max Edelson put it, the slaves remade the landscape to suit the rice crop—digging ditches and laying out

10. The inventory is a composite, for we do not know what was actually on Hutchenson's shelves. See Darrett B. Rutman and Anita H. Rutman, *A Place in Time: Middlesex Country, Virginia, 1650–1750* (New York: Norton, 1984), 205–207; Stephanie Grauman Wolf, *As Various as Their Land: Everyday Lives of Eighteenth-Century Americans* (New York: HarperCollins, 1993), 191; Sharon V. Sallinger, *Taverns and Drinking in Early America* (Baltimore: Johns Hopkins University Press, 2002), 196; Breen, *Marketplace of Revolution*, 118 and after.

11. J. H. Elliott, *Empires of the Atlantic World: Britain and Spain in America, 1492–1830* (New Haven, Conn.: Yale University Press, 2006), 282; Wood, *Black Majority*, 59, 61–62; James Glen (1760), quoted in *American Negro Slavery*, by U. B. Phillips (New York: Appleton, 1918), 89.

embankments, "the construction and maintenance of reservoirs, canals, water gates, and ponds." For the key to Low Country rice was the "command of water." Too much water ruined the crop; too little killed it. Using "comparatively simple" manipulation of the landscape, involving a dam, a drainage ditch, a "water stop," the skilled slaves among the workers could "throw water" on the rice then drain the fields. The water-saturated soil in the wetlands turned to "puff mud" with the consistency of quicksand.[12]

Rice cultivation was back-breaking year-round work. As the Charles Town doctor Alexander Garden recalled, slaves were always busy "tilling, planting, hoeing, reaping, threshing, and pounding" the rice crop. Early winter was a time of preparation: ditches had to be cleared and gates and sluices repaired in time for the early-spring planting of the seedlings. Later the fields

---

12. S. Max Edelson, *Plantation Enterprise in Colonial South Carolina* (Cambridge, Mass.: Harvard University Press, 2006), 76, 104–105. S. Max Edelson agrees with David Eltis, Philip Morgan, and David Richardson that slaves from African rice-producing regions did not play the crucial role in the takeoff of rice culture in South Carolina. Without the market that the planters and their mercantile agents in Britain created, rice would not have been nearly so profitable. Peter Wood, Gwendolin Medlo-Hall, Judith Carney, and Daniel Littlefield disagree. They believe that slaves from rice-producing coastal regions in West Africa made a major contribution at a critical time. "Driving this debate is an underlying disagreement about whether or not slaves exerted significant influence on economic formation in South Carolina, and by implication throughout the Americas." Edelson, "Beyond 'Black Rice': Reconstructing Material and Cultural Contexts for Early Plantation Agriculture," *American Historical Review* 115 (2010), 135. See their essays in the "AHR Exchange: The Question of Black Rice," *American Historical Review* 115 (2010), 123–171. But no one denies the agency of the slaves or the crucial contribution they made to the entire enterprise.

had to be covered with water, then drained and hoed, then covered again, until by the end of summer the rice plants could be harvested, reaped, tied into sheaves, and carried to the threshing yard. Whole-rice grain was shipped to market, while broken grain was eaten. All of the field work was slave labor; when not tending the rice, slaves planted food crops; grew, harvested, and prepared indigo (a dye); cut wood; and did the endless round of tasks every farm required.[13]

By 1739 the rice planters had adopted inland cultivation, extending plantations from the coast. The slaves of the fortunate planters whose fields bordered navigable rivers, such as the Cooper or Edisto, could efficiently transport the rice barrels from the pounding site to the dock. From there, sloops or pettigers (small, flat-bottomed boats) or schooners would navigate to Charleston or other markets. For those planters farther from navigable water, their slaves would have to transport the barrels by wagon on local roads or turnpikes to the closest public dock.

The rice went to Charles Town, where merchant exporters like Pringle managed the colonial side of the commerce and speculated on crop futures. In August 1739, shortly before the Stono uprising, he wrote to John Richards, a London commodities broker, "We have a good prospect for a large crop of rice, and if the season continues to be favorable we shall have a very large quantity of rice again this year." The only danger was the prospect of

13. Alexander Garden (1755) quoted in Michael J. Heitzler, *Goose Creek: A Definitive History* (Charleston: The History Press, 2005), 1:175; J. H. Easterby, ed., "Introduction," *The South Carolina Rice Plantation, As Revealed in the Papers of Robert F. W. Allston* (Chicago: University of Chicago Press, 1945), 33; rice tour, Middleton Place Museum, Charleston, S.C.

a war with Spain, but Pringle supposed that would not interrupt the shipping of rice. Nothing must interrupt the flow of rice. To his brother William, Pringle wrote to ask he send more rum—"as there is always a great consumption of same," for after all, drinking the water would kill anyone, and he added, "We shall have a very large crop of rice this year."[14]

The rice trade would have been impossible without the acuity and competitiveness of London bankers and Scottish "factors" who offered credit and facilitated warehousing and transshipping of the colonial crops, or of eager ship captains and supercargoes who participated in the slave trade on the African coast, though it might cost them half their crews to tropical diseases. Most of all, the rice trade could not have prospered without the capital accumulation of the planters themselves, doubling from 1722 to the eve of the American Revolution. For the planters did what every capitalist must do—reinvest the returns in the business: more land under cultivation, more slave labor, more rice, more profit.[15]

The rice trade made South Carolina a jewel of the British Empire. Crop production zoomed between 1720 and 1740, exports increasing from 8.2 million pounds a year to 35 million. Marketed aggressively and ably by the British, Carolina

14. Pringle to John Richards, August 3, 1739; Pringle to Nathaniel French, August 20, 1739; Pringle to William Pringle, August 21, 1739, in *The Letterbook of Robert Pringle*, ed. Walter B. Edgar (Columbia: University of South Carolina Press, 1972), 1:121–123.

15. Bernard Bailyn, *Atlantic History: Concept and Contours* (Cambridge, Mass.: Harvard University Press, 2005), 84; Peter A. Coclanis, *The Shadow of a Dream: Economic Life and Death in the South Carolina Low Country, 1670–1920* (New York: Oxford University Press, 1989), 95.

rice replaced other non-British sources of the foodstuff. South Carolina rice fed slaves in the Caribbean, workers in England, Mediterranean sailors, and Dutch families. By the end of the colonial period, rice was the third most valuable export from the mainland United States.[16]

Innovation went hand in hand with the success of rice cultivation. Ideas of personal improvement, the sciences, and the progress of society permeated the Atlantic world. The ideas traveled in books and magazines and newspapers, part of every cargo from England into Charles Town. The planters' mansions featured libraries, and planters were proud of their role in the modernization of agriculture. They believed in progress, for in fact they were the cutting edge of a brave new world of productivity and material improvement. According to the historian Joyce Chaplin, "Lowcountry planters, who had the most successful form of agriculture, nevertheless restlessly tinkered with new crops and machines.... [T]hey had the strongest connections to the modernizing, commercial world." When native rice plants proved unprofitable, they introduced new varieties. When hand labor in threshing and pounding the rice proved too time consuming, they introduced mechanical substitutes. When Indian slaves proved unreliable, the planters tapped into the Atlantic supply of African slaves.[17]

16. R. C. Nash, "South Carolina in the Atlantic Economy in the Late Seventeenth and Eighteenth Centuries," *Economic History Review* 45 (1992), 679–680; Coclanis, *Shadow of a Dream*, 53.

17. Joyce Chaplin, *An Anxious Pursuit: Agricultural Innovation and Modernity in the Lower South, 1730–1815* (Chapel Hill: University of North Carolina Press, 1993), 183.

Hutchenson's store was also a warehouse for the goods in the Indian trade. From Charles Town, merchants reached out to the Creek and other Indian peoples to the west, seeking deerskins and other commodities of the forest. Indians traded these for firearms, cookware, clothing, and other consumer durables, and for alcoholic beverages. Agents of the merchants lived in the Indians' towns part of the year, which was acceptable to the natives as long as the traders followed native customs. But the traders were not always scrupulous in their dealings with their hosts. This was particularly true in that other trade—the trade in human flesh—that profited the Charles Town merchants. Merchants made the Indians into active partners in the slave trade, encouraging them to raid other Indians' villages and sell the captives.[18]

At the store, planters and servants rubbed elbows with newcomers from England, Scotland, and Wales; with French-speaking Huguenots and German pietists; with middle-aged men hoping to start over and young men hoping to get rich quick. Poorer farmers, just making ends meet, sought credit from the storekeepers, and better-established planters spoke for their less-well-to-do neighbors. No one cosigned notes for small purchases (major purchases were another matter), for a man's word was either good or it was not, though merchants would mark up prices when a purchaser's credit was suspect. These white men dealt with one another in a rough equality, but everyone knew

18. Alan Gallay, *The Indian Slave Trade: The Rise of the English Empire in the American South, 1670–1717* (New Haven, Conn.: Yale University Press, 2003), 357; James H. Merrell, *The Indians' New World: Catawbas and Their Neighbors from European Contact through the Era of Removal* (Chapel Hill: University of North Carolina Press, 1989), 91.

their place. The poor white man balanced his fierce sense of personal independence with the knowledge that he would always be dependent on his social and economic superiors for loans, for jobs, and for help at the courts in Charles Town. In their turn, the well-to-do knew that their honor and reputation rested upon the support of their social and economic inferiors.[19]

Topics of conversation ran to weather, crop futures, complaints about the indolence and insolence of slaves, boasting about horses, and tidbits of information about who was sick from which of the many diseases endemic to the Low Country. Local and colonial politics was another subject of interest, for South Carolina had, among the colonies, the largest percentage of free white male voters. Elections for the lower house of the legislature were not hotly contested, however. People in the parishes knew who the most important men were and deferred to them at election time.[20]

If South Carolina Low Country society was a hierarchy, with niches well defined by wealth and status, gender and race, it was a truncated hierarchy. Once the original proprietary grantees had sold off their huge original grants, there were no great nobles. Status was not based on lineage but on wealth. A family might ascend to or descend from the top rank within a single generation. Because so much of the land was vacant (a term that the surveyors used to describe the land plats) or unclaimed, station in society

19. Olwell, *Masters, Slaves, and Subjects*, 34–35; Martin, *Buying into the World of Goods*, 20.
20. Richard Beeman, *The Varieties of Political Experience in Eighteenth-Century America* (Philadelphia: University of Pennsylvania Press, 2004), 37, 127, 138.

Fenwick Hall (1730), Johns Island, wings added later (photograph by author).

was always uncertain. It depended on how others saw a person's status. To act beneath one's station brought shame; to ignore disrespect to one's station brought dishonor.[21]

But South Carolina's remained an anxious gentility. For a man might pose as a gentleman, maintaining his honor by offering assistance to those below him in rank, but in the end status depended upon wealth, and wealth depended on forces that the planter could not control. Good fortune or ill depended upon the price of rice in the Atlantic market, the marketing and financial

21. Bertram Wyatt-Brown, *Southern Honor: Ethics and Behavior in the Old South* (New York: Oxford University Press, 1982), 88–89.

skills of people thousands of miles away, the weather, and perhaps most precarious, the control of slave labor. The master portrayed himself as the good father, the head of an extended household, in which slaves were childlike laborers, women were submissive helpmeets, and servants were obedient and loyal. Masters could put on a stern face, like the biblical patriarchs, or act the loving and affectionate father, an increasingly popular pose in eighteenth-century polite English society. However he handled sentiment and authority, the planter was an anxious man.[22]

❦

For, in fact, successful planters were not gentlemen of leisure. They were aggressive businessmen. They speculated in land and slaves, buying, selling, trading, always looking for some advantage. Parcels of land changed hands rapidly, as speculation in land ran a close second to actually cultivating the land as a source of wealth. They borrowed money and loaned money, and kept account books on every penny that came in and went out.[23]

So-called memorials, land surveys required by law after 1731 that traced ownership back to the original grants, show a patchwork of individual farms. Some were no more than a hundred acres. Most were in the 200- to 1,000-acre range. The patchwork was not a quilt, however, for the plats were too irregular. Instead, they zigzagged. The watercourses dictated curves, and prior grants required short stretches of stakes sharply cutting at acute angles.

---

22. Kathleen Brown, *Good Wives, Nasty Wenches, and Anxious Patriarchs: Gender, Race, and Power in Colonial Virginia* (Chapel Hill: University of North Carolina Press, 1996), 322.

23. Edelson, *Plantation Enterprise*, 95.

For example, Thomas Elliott's grant of 524 acres in Colleton was a giant horseshoe, part swamp, along one of the many creeks that cut the savannah and swamp into pieces. Another grant of 580 acres lay along the Pon Pon River in the St. Bartholomew Parish of Colleton. The Elliotts bought and sold parcels in addition to cultivating them, married into other planter families, served the county in a variety of capacities, and made money on rice.[24]

White women also came to Hutchenson's. The store did not stock as many decorative or ornamental items as the big shops in Charles Town, but on the shelves were buttons and threads, fabrics and ribbons and buckles. And what good were these without "looking glasses"? By the middle of the century, women routinely ordered from merchants' books what was not in stock. More and more of the planters' household income, even for plain farm folks at the edge of the settlements, was devoted to consumer durable items for domestic comfort, such as porcelain flatware, cookware, eating utensils, clothing, and home furnishings.[25]

Wives and daughters, planning visits to one another, determined much of the household's outlay for consumer goods. For the newly expanded planter's home design, with its parlors and sitting rooms, women wanted cushioned chairs and wallpaper. Visitors were entitled to comfort. In the sitting room, the women engaged in polite conversation. Alone, the planter's wife or daugh-

24. Thomas Elliott surveys, 1734, plat book, S213184, South Carolina Department of Archives and History [SCDAH], Columbia, S.C.

25. Edward Pearson, "Planters Full of Money," in *Money, Trade, and Power: The Evolution of South Carolina's Plantation Society*, ed. Jack P. Greene, Rosemary Brana-Shute, and Randy J. Sparks (Columbia: University of South Carolina Press, 2001), 309.

ter would read the newest novels and essays from Britain, just arrived at the store. Or they would write letters. The mark of gentility was fine handwriting and polite conversation. Much of that correspondence and conversation concerned the health of family members and concern for loved ones missing at sea, abroad, or away on business. Women's thoughts also extended to material goods. Women of lower status might not be able to write (though most could read a bit), but even the meanest cabin treasured some pewter plates or a Delftware serving piece.[26]

Patriarchal assumptions about women's subordinate place, reinforced by the English common law, denied women a separate identity from their husbands, restricting women's roles. In law, a married woman could not control her own property or buy or sell without her husband's consent. But disease and distance undid what the law sought to impose. Unmarried women and widows could own land and manage plantations in the countryside and run businesses in Charles Town. The widows Ann Drayton and Ann Elliott were two of the largest landowners on Johns Island. Widows and daughters bought and sold, rented out, and leased slaves; managed plantations; and kept account books. Such women did not identify along gender lines with black women but with their own white male relations.[27]

26. David Shields, *Civil Tongues and Polite Letters in British America* (Chapel Hill: University of North Carolina Press, 1997), 54; Bushman, *Refinement of America*, 30–46, 122, 151–153. Ian K. Steele, *The English Atlantic 1675–1740: An Exploration of Communication and Community* (New York: Oxford University Press, 1986), documents the Atlantic transit of manners and information.

27. Cara Anzilotti, *In the Affairs of the World: Women, Patriarchy, and Power in Colonial South Carolina* (Westport, Conn.: Greenwood, 2002), 54–55.

Women such as young Eliza Lucas, manager of her absent father's three plantations, found life not unpleasant. In 1740 she wrote to an English correspondent, "[I] think Carolina greatly preferable to the West Indies [where she was born and lived until her fifteenth year].... Charles Town, the principal one in this province, is a polite, agreeable place. The people live very gentile and very much in the English taste. The Country is in general fertile.... We are 17 miles by land and 6 by water from Charles Town—where we have about 6 agreeable families round us with whom we live in great harmony." Surrounded by English, Welsh, and Scottish planters, with enough land and slaves to make her life comfortable, Eliza was proud that she had "the business of 3 plantations to transact, which requires much writing and more business and fatigue of other sorts than you can imagine." When she needed store-bought supplies, she sent to Charles Town or visited the shops there herself.[28]

Offices in the back of stores like Hutchenson's were filled with account books, slips of paper that waited to be recorded in the ledger, correspondence, and personal items. Records were kept, but rarely was the bookkeeping a model of accounting practices. Even the major merchants of Philadelphia and elsewhere kept sloppy books. The customers bought on credit, the records appearing as "book debt" in the ledgers. Debtors could work off what they owed by bartering labor or goods. In such face-to-

28. Eliza Lucas to Mrs. Boddicott, May 2, 1740, *The Letterbook of Eliza Lucas Pinckney, 1739–1762*, ed. Elise Pinckney (Chapel Hill: University of North Carolina Press, 1972), 6–7.

face situations, a person's reputation was the surest guarantee of repayment, and customers were very aware of the need to maintain a good reputation. The bankrupt was a shame as well as a material loss.[29]

Bankruptcy lurked around the corner for everyone who traded at Hutchenson's; hence the need for planters to bring more acres under cultivation, the search for alternative money-making crops, and the demand for more slaves. And like quicksand, in which the agitated efforts of a trapped animal causes it to sink further, increasing production drove down prices, and lower prices meant a narrower profit margin. The trap was inescapable and the laws by which it operated were part and parcel of the international market.

❧

A land of sharp and sometimes disturbing natural contrasts, of long sunny growing seasons and devastating storms, of swaths of primeval forest crisscrossed by heavily cultivated rice fields, South Carolina was a magnet for entrepreneurs and a hell for laborers. Although it was still a young society in 1739, planters, yeoman farmers, tenants, and slaves already knew their place. The Low Country lived and thrived, or withered and died, according to the fortunes of rice, and rice cultivation's profitability depended ultimately on the operation of markets in Britain, the Mediterranean, and the Caribbean. Still, there would have been no South Carolina rice to sell or buy without slaves. South Carolina Low Country was slave country.

29. On merchant practices, see Naomi R. Lamoreaux, "Rethinking the Transition to Capitalism in the Early American Northeast," *Journal of American History* 90 (September 2003), 437–461.

· *Two* ·

INHUMAN BONDAGE

Slaves came to Hutchenson's store. Some bought for their masters' larder or sold items for their masters' profit. Masters sometimes rewarded slaves with cash or allowed them to peddle their labor on the market. Sometimes the slaves did not act for or with the permission of their masters. In 1696 the assembly warned that "if any free man or free woman at any time…shall buy, sell, bargain, contract, barter or exchange any manner of goods and commodities whatsoever, to, for, or with any servant or servants, slave or slaves, without the privity [knowledge] or consent of their master, mistress, or overseers, he, she, or they so offending…shall satisfy and pay ten times the value of such goods" to the other party, and return the goods to their original owner. But the law never stopped the black market in goods, so commonly was it practiced. In January 1738 the Carolina Assembly was still debating how to frame "a bill for licensing hawkers, pedlars, and petty chapmen to prevent their trading with Negroes or other slaves."[1]

---

1. "An Act Prohibiting the trading with Servants and Slaves," March 16, 1696, in John D. Cushing, ed., *Earliest Printed Laws of South Carolina,*

Without slaves, Carolina would never have been profitable enough to merit colonization. With slaves, no planter ever rested wholly secure in his bed. Slaves were property in law, but every slave and every planter knew the contrary. Slaves were men and women and children, each different, each an individual. Such contradictions twisted the laws every which way. When some legislators wanted to mandate the execution of runaway slaves, the majority of the Commons demurred. Was that because a runaway was still a valuable piece of property, or because masters and slaves knew that many runaways simply ran from a cruel new owner back to a decent former master? Why require that slave fishermen pay five pounds colony money a year for a license when slaves were not allowed to own boats? Was it because slave fishermen were very able, and fish plentiful in the creeks, rivers, and along the ocean shore? The assemblymen refused to deny to slaves the practice of going to market for their masters, whatever liberties this allowed the slave to trade on the side for himself.[2]

In spite of the internal contradictions in the institution of slavery and the dangers of slave resistance, the planter rulers of Carolina wedded themselves to bound labor from the founding of the colony. While the proprietors to whom Charles II gave the vast territory that would become North and South Carolina sat in English manor houses, the first settlers set out from Barbados,

---

1692–1734 (Wilmington, Del.: Glazier, 1978), 52; *Journal of the Commons House of Assembly, November 10, 1736–June 7, 1739,* January 23, 1738, p. 420.

2. *Journal of the Commons House of Assembly, November 10, 1736–June 7, 1739,* January 26, 1738, p. 428; March 6, 1738, p. 512.

bringing their slaves with them. To accommodate these sugar planters, the ideal constitution for the proprietary colony of Carolina that the proprietor Anthony Ashley Cooper's secretary, John Locke, penned provided for the absolute dominion of master over slave. "No slave" was to be exempted from the "civil dominion his master hath over him," even if the slave were a Christian.[3]

The rice plantations on both sides of the Stono River teemed with slaves. A few were Native Americans. Most were African in origin. Some of the latter had come by way of the British sugar islands of Barbados, Jamaica, St. Christopher, and Antigua. But labor there was so valuable and slaves' life expectancy so short that the islands could spare few slaves for the mainland colonies. Those that did come were always suspected of having been sent to Carolina after harboring murderous designs against their masters or the slave traders. So, by the 1720s the vast majority of slaves were imported directly from the west coast of Africa.[4]

Importation from Africa to South Carolina in the eighteenth century far exceeded imports to the other mainland colonies, including those of the Chesapeake. From 1700 to 1776 some 93,000 enslaved men and women were brought from Africa directly to Charles Town, 35,000 of them arriving before 1750. Between 1730 and 1744, nearly 75 percent of these came from the chiefdoms of

3. John Locke, "Fundamental Constitutions," 1669, in *Works of John Locke* (Longman: London, 1824), 9:196 (article 107).

4. Marcus Rediker, *The Slave Ship: A Human History* (New York: Viking, 2007), 35; Gregory E. O'Malley, "Beyond the Middle Passage: Slave Migration from the Caribbean to North America, 1619–1807," *William and Mary Quarterly*, 3rd ser., 66 (January 2009), 125–172.

Angola and Kongo. Such an imbalance (the numbers far exceeding those from farther north on the West African coast) suggests that the colony's planters preferred slaves from those regions.[5]

Recent scholarly attention to the details of the Atlantic slave trade allow greater precision in documenting South Carolina's slave importation. From averaging around 600 newcomers a year in the 1720s, the number of imported slaves shot above 2,500 a year on average in the 1730s. In 1731, slave traders carried 1,766 slaves (mostly men) to the colony, or at least those were the slaves on whom the importers paid the legal duty. The real number would have been higher. By 1735, slave imports had risen to 2,907 souls, and in 1736 more than 3,500 bondmen and women entered the colony. Even these figures are based on the payment of slave-import duties—so the number of slaves actually arriving exceeded the recorded figure. Slaves coming directly from Africa were briefly quarantined on Sullivan's Island, east of Charles Town, but most were sold to planters within two weeks of their arrival in the New World either through prior consignment or at auction. The *South Carolina Gazette* advertised every shipment of these "choice Negroes" to be sold at auction.[6]

5. David Richardson, "The British Slave Trade to Colonial South Carolina," *Slavery and Abolition* 12 (December 1991), 129, 137.

6. Peter Wood, *Black Majority: Negroes in Colonial South Carolina through the Stono Rebellion* (New York: Norton, 1973), 149–151; Peter A. Coclanis, *The Shadow of a Dream: Economic Life and Death in the South Carolina Low Country, 1670–1920* (New York: Oxford University Press, 1989), 45; Russell Menard, "Slave Demography in the Low Country, 1670–1748," *South Carolina Magazine of History* 96 (1995), 295; *South Carolina Gazette*, June 9, 1739, p. 3; Philip Morgan, *Slave Counterpoint: Black Culture in the Eighteenth-Century Chesapeake and Low Country* (Chapel Hill: University of North Carolina Press, 1998), 73–75.

By 1738 the demand for slaves had reached a new high. In 1738 the *Seaflower* arrived in Charles Town—217 slaves had embarked, and 217 were delivered—a perfect record of cargo handling, and not easy, when the cargo was packed into the hold like sardines, sanitation was minimal (hence dysentery and typhus were rife), and slaves sometimes preferred suicide to the fate awaiting them at the end of the journey. Slaves of different nationalities might even fight one another. The *Shepherd* arrived soon after, its original cargo of 396 slaves reduced during the voyage to 360. The *Amoretta* made port the next year with even worse luck: of the 258 slaves taken aboard in the Bight of Biafra, only 207 survived the middle passage of the voyage; this mortality rate was higher than the 10 percent a slaver in the mid-eighteenth century might expect. But nothing stopped the trade into Charles Town. The *Shepherd* was back in 1739, returning once again with a cargo from Loango on the Kongo coast of Central West Africa. Captain Maurice Power loaded 373 slaves, of whom 339 lived to see Charles Town harbor. In 1739, a total of 1,702 slaves were reported coming into the colony—a figure that would have been higher but for the rumors of war with Spain affecting shipping in the Caribbean. From the trade, successful captains could become quite wealthy. Crews did not fare so well. Nearly a quarter died from tropical diseases or other causes during the voyages.[7]

Without the highly visible cooperation of whites and blacks, the English colonization of South Carolina would have been stillborn. The first slaves the Barbadian planters brought to South

7. Transatlantic Slave Trade Database; www.slavevoyages.org/tast/assessment/estimates.faces; Rediker, *Slave Ship*, 295.

Carolina had a good deal of freedom in the new colony. Enslaved men turned the tidal lowlands between the Ashley and the Cooper rivers into Charles Town. Slaves served as "pioneers," clearing land and watching over herds of cattle. Africans who had experience with rice culture in their homelands helped transform the coastal areas into rice plantations, some of which were as wealthy as any agricultural complexes in the Western world. Owners left slaves to their tasks without much supervision. But such freedom was a matter of exigency and practicality, not law. Slaves always knew they were slaves. As more and more slaves entered the colony and the ratio of slaves to whites shifted to a slave majority, the fears of whites grew and the relative independence of blacks shrank. For the development of plantation rice culture left whites increasingly isolated in a sea of imported African slaves. By 1740 the colony's population ratio was 2.6 slaves to 1 free person.[8]

For the whites, control of the slave population was a necessity, and South Carolina's masters had a relatively easy way to identify the slave. Slaves were dark-skinned. The concept of racial differences (and consequently racism) was not yet fully developed in Western thought, but apologists for a slavery had already developed a color scheme. White was morally pure, noble, innocent, heroic, close to godly. Black was morally debased, lazy, cowardly, and close to the wild animal. The leading seventeenth-century authority on international law, including the law of slavery, Samuel von Pufendorf, proposed in 1672 that some races of men

8. Wood, *Black Majority*, 34–35, 36–62, 95–130, 131–166; John J. McCusker and Russell R. Menard, *The Economy of British America, 1607–1789*, rev. ed. (Chapel Hill: University of North Carolina Press, 1991), 174–185.

were by their inherent nature so stupid that they were not fit to govern themselves. Enslaved, however, they had the good fortune "to live in subjection to a wise director [and] without doubt fixed in such a state of life as is most agreeable to their genius and capacity." By 1739 the slave traders and the planters who bought the men and women off the ships in Charles Town had rationalized their actions according to physical and cultural differences—Africans were suited by nature and God to serve the planters.[9]

The first Virginia laws—the first laws in the British colonies on the subject—distinguished slaves from servants on the basis of color. For example, "whereas the frequent meetings of considerable numbers of Negro slaves under pretense of feasts and burials is judged of dangerous consequence," slaves at such gatherings were not to carry firearms. "These two words, *Negro* and *Slave*" were "by custom grown homogenous and convertible," one Virginia clergyman wrote in 1680. In 1702 the New York legislature provided for summary trials of slaves accused of assaulting "white women." The South Carolina slave code of 1740 pronounced that any slave striking or attempting to strike "a white person" was guilty of a serious offense.[10]

9. Samuel von Pufendorf, *Of the Law of Nature and Nations* [1672], quoted in *An Inquiry into the Law of Negro Slavery in the United States of America* [1858], by T. R. R. Cobb, ed. Paul Finkelman (Athens: University of Georgia Press, 1999), 19. On the science of racism, see William R. Stanton, *The Leopard's Spots: Scientific Attitudes toward Race in America, 1815–1859* (Chicago: University of Chicago Press, 1960), and George M. Frederickson, *Racism: A Short History* (Princeton: Princeton University Press, 2002).

10. The following citations and the accompanying text first appeared, in somewhat different fashion and context, in my *Sensory Worlds in Early America* (Baltimore: Johns Hopkins University Press, 2003), 137–149:

So important was color to the definition of slavery that the storekeeper and his white patrons at Hutchenson's were self-appointed experts on variations of slave color. As Thomas R. R. Cobb, the premier antebellum apologist of American slavery, would write in 1858, "The black color alone does not constitute the Negro…there are a great number of tribes, differing not so much in their physical as moral nature, and adapting them more or less for a state of servitude. This difference was well known among the native tribes long before the Dutch, Portuguese, and English vied with each other in extending the slave trade." The faux science of colors told the potential purchaser of slaves at the auction houses that Angolans were dark and amiable but slow-witted; men and women from the Gambia River area were light-skinned and hard-working but rebellious. The people of the Bight of Biafra, stereotyped by the planter–importers as yellow-ish in hue, were less desirable than any other group, for suppos-edly they were prone to suicide.[11]

Masters employed a myriad of words to describe the shades of the unfree men and women—some taken from the spectrum

---

Virginia Slave Law of 1680, quoted in *In the Matter of Color: Race and the American Legal Process, the Colonial Period*, by A. Leon Higginbotham (New York: Oxford University Press, 1978), 39; Morgan Godwyn, quoted in *Southern Slavery and the Law, 1619–1860*, by Thomas D. Morris (Chapel Hill: University of North Carolina Press, 1996), 17; Julius Goebel Jr. and T. Raymond Naughton, *Law Enforcement in Colonial New York: A Study in Criminal Procedure* (New York: Commonwealth Fund, 1944), 418.

11. Cobb, *Inquiry into the Law of Negro Slavery*, 22–23; David C. Littlefield, *Rice and Slaves: Ethnicity and the Slave Trade in Colonial South Carolina* (Baton Rouge: Louisiana State University Press, 1981), 8–21, 25, 31, 73.

(purple, deepest black, dark brownish, yellow), others of cultural origin (mulatto, quadroon, Negro). Newspaper advertisements for runaway slaves in South Carolina, a fixture in the *Charles-Town Gazette* and just about every other colonial newspaper, were prosaic and explicit on color. Phyllis was a "mustee" woman who ran from her South Carolina master in 1732. She, like other mustee slaves, might have been mistaken for an Indian. Juno, who took flight the next year, was "of the blackest color," and three lately arrived Angolans, "Hector, Peter, and Dublin...[were] of very black complexions." Time in America, and proximity to their masters, extended the palette of slave hues: one clerk's record depicted men and women of African ancestry as "very dark, dark mulatto, black, yellow, copper, high mulatto, dark brown, fair, freckled, bright, high bright, light, light brown, and not very black."[12]

The encounter between slave and free at Hutchenson's involved speaking and listening in addition to looking and seeing. The slaves at Hutchenson's had to learn to communicate with the white population. The varying accents of English—the drawl of the immigrants from southern England, the nasal twang of the northern English, the burr of the Scots and the Irish, the broken English of the French Huguenots, and the guttural English

12. Robert E. Desrochers Jr., "Slave-for-Sale Advertisements and Slavery in Massachusetts, 1704–1781," *William and Mary Quarterly*, 3d ser., 59 (July 2002), 623–664; Lathan A. Windley, ed., *Runaway Slave Advertisements, A Documentary History from the 1730s to 1790, Volume 3: South Carolina* (Westport, Conn. Greenwood, 1983), 3:2, 7, 8; Edward L. Ayers, *In the Presence of Mine Enemies: War in the Heart of America, 1859–1863* (New York: Norton, 2003), 21.

of the Germans—all posed challenges to the most attentive of slave ears. And the slaves themselves spoke a myriad of tongues. The Bantu dialects of Angola were as different from the Yoruba of the Nigerians as Italian is from Finnish. Masters and slaves thus had to learn to talk to one another in pidgins composed of native idioms and English. Among themselves, to be sure, slaves' "deepest prayers and desires were expressed through their mother tongue."[13]

Masters used renaming to control slaves, dubbing them with classical, English, or biblical names. But many slaves forced a compromise. Slaves retained their public or "day names" that corresponded to the days of the week. Cudjoe and Juba were the male and female Akan (roughly, modern Ghana) day names for Monday. Quaco and Cuba were the equivalents for Wednesday. Cuffee and Quibba were Friday names, and Quashee and Quashiba were Sunday. Sometimes an African name was written as a classical Greek or Roman name merely because it sounded the same, hence Cato for the Yoruba (roughly, modern southwestern Nigerian) Keta. Sometimes place of origin was added as a surrogate for a family name, like Congo Tom, or Coromantu Cubba (Coromanti was a Gold Coast town). The acculturation allowed slaves to recall old sounds. Even when these were changed again,

13. Wood, *Black Majority*, 172–186; Morgan, *Slave Counterpoint*, 562–580; Maureen Warner Lewis, "The African Impact on Language and Literature in the English Speaking Caribbean: Continued Existence of African Languages, A Case Study of Yoruba in Trinidad," in *Africa and the Caribbean: The Legacies of a Link*, ed. Margaret E. Graham and Franklin W. Knight (Baltimore: Johns Hopkins University Press, 1979), 104.

Anglicized, as was Jack for Quaco, Joe for Cudjoe, and Coffee for Cuffee, the slave could sound out the old word.[14]

Slaves kept from masters another name—the secret name that African parents gave their children. Just so, slaves sometimes manipulated what they said to whites to create space and time away from the master's intrusive eye. Landon Carter, a Chesapeake planter, kept a diary in which he featured his dealings with his slaves. It reveals how often he felt exasperated by the extent to which slaves found ways to excuse their absenteeism and negligence on the plantations. Mangorike Willy, Simon the ox-carter, and Bart deflected Carter's fury by playing on words, telling stories about other slaves, and feigning either childlike contrition or simple stupidity. The masters were well aware of the slaves' verbal games and carried on their own side of the contest by teaching slaves English, requiring polite responses, and both rewarding and punishing slaves according to the nature of their speaking and listening. Some slaves were allowed to say more than others,

14. Wood, *Black Majority*, 172–191; Michael Craton, *Searching for the Invisible Man: Slaves and Plantation Life in Jamaica* (Cambridge, Mass.: Harvard University Press, 1978), 55, 59, 157; Joseph E. Holloway, *Africanisms in American Culture* (Bloomington: Indiana University Press, 2005), 85; Jerome S. Handler and JoAnn Jacoby, "Slave Names and Naming in Barbados, 1650–1830," *William and Mary Quarterly*, 3rd ser., 53 (1996), 685–729. Allan Kulikoff has told the author that few of these names survived the first generation, at least in the Chesapeake. He concedes that his findings are based on slave masters' estate inventories, however, and that this source might underreport the number of African slaves that kept their old names and passed them on without the master's explicit consent. What is more, in South Carolina, where slaves usually lived among other slaves, African names would have persisted longer than in the Chesapeake, his area of study, where slaves had far more contact with free persons.

or excused for speaking out of turn, but the verbal jousting went on continuously.[15]

Should they meet at the store or on the road, slaves were expected to address whites in a deferential manner. The "saucy" or disrespectful slave could be corrected, even struck, by a white person without incurring any legal liability. Thus, slave speech was often slurred, or mumbled, or spoken with a glance to the side or down. This was a defense mechanism the enslaved learned in Africa, where it was a sign of respect for young people to avoid meeting the gaze of their elders.[16]

When slaves spoke to one another, their voices took on greater animation. In Charles Town, slave conversations in shops and on the street were far more relaxed than conversations with their masters. The slave speakers "saturated the landscape" with distinctive cadences and tones, a music of speech. Listening was as important as speaking. Able slave storytellers were much admired within the slave quarters. There, African themes and Carolina scenes blended together in a rich combination of satire, parable, and instruction.[17]

15. Rhys Isaac, *The Transformation of Virginia, 1749–1790* (Chapel Hill: University of North Carolina Press, 1979), 340–341.

16. *Virginia Gazette*, November 14–21, 1745; *Virginia Gazette*, October 28–November 4, 1737; *Virginia Gazette*, May 15, 1752. I am grateful to Thomas M. Costa and Harold Gill for calling these references to my attention. The "down look" was common enough among slaves but was not as common as masters imagined. Shane White and Graham White, *Stylin': African American Expressive Culture from its Beginnings to the Zoot Suit* (Ithaca, N.Y.: Cornell University Press, 1998), 68–69. The slave might also try on a "roguish down look" or a "sneaking down look."

17. Graham White and Shane White, *The Sounds of Slavery* (Boston: Beacon, 2005), 95–96; Mark M. Smith, *Listening to Nineteenth-Century America* (Chapel Hill: University of North Carolina Press, 2001), 68.

Masters sometimes permitted slaves to gather for funerals, parties, and other communal events away from the plantation. The noise level at one of these was so loud that one white passerby complained that slaves were "great and loud talkers." Slaves' voices were most apparent to whites when men and women joined in song and dance, common occurrences in slave communities. Songs often had an African cadence and tonality, even if the words were English. At mock elections presided over by slaves in New England and New York, musicians dressed in outlandish costumes, played drums, horns, and stringed instruments, and marched ahead of feather- and jewel-bedecked "kings." Slave onlookers added their own noise to the parade. Sound expressed emotion, joy and sorrow, through "shouting and clapping hands and singing."[18]

Some masters respected a quasi privacy of valued slaves in the quarters, allowing them to live and work without much supervision. Other respected slaves, such as house servants, lived in or near the dwelling house of their master. Slaves who grew up in a household might develop some affection for a kind master and his family. One must understand that such affection was not a

18. Quoted in Morgan, *Slave Counterpoint*, 122; Mechal Sobel, *The World They Made Together: Black and White Values in Eighteenth-Century Virginia* (Princeton: Princeton University Press, 1987), 141–142; Eugene Genovese, *Roll Jordan Roll: The World the Slaves Made* (New York: Pantheon, 1974), 199, 324; William D. Piersen, *Black Yankees: The Creation of an African American Subculture in Eighteenth-Century New England* (Amherst: University of Massachusetts Press, 1988), 121–122; Fannie Berry, recalling the aural celebration of freedom at Appomattox Court House in April 1865, quoted in *Making Whiteness: The Culture of Segregation in the South, 1890–1940*, by Grace Elizabeth Hale (New York: Pantheon, 1998), 1.

Alice Huger Smith, Taking Seed Rice Down to the Fields *(Gibbes Museum, Charleston).*

constant emotion or a permanent bond but a feeling that could come and go. Affection always has that character.

Conscience might exaggerate a master's belief in this affection. Henry Laurens, who had no love of slavery himself though he was a leading slave trader, reported that when he returned from a long trip abroad, his old domestic slaves welcomed him with tears and embraces. He reciprocated. The scene had a literary touch—perhaps Laurens had recalled Odysseus returning to Ithaca, but at the very least the slaves recognized a kind master when they saw one. For the slave, a show of affection was part of the process of negotiation and manipulation, a tool that slaves could use to mitigate the harshness of bondage. But the affection might be genuine. As the North Carolina slave Moses Grandy wrote, years later, slaves and whites who spent childhood together could, on occasion, forget their respective stations. A 1737 issue of the Charleston, South Carolina, *Gazette* reported that a youth traveling with a young slave down the Ashley River to start school in Charles Town had drowned. The two, dead, were later found in one another's embrace—the slave trying to save the master's son, the son clinging to the slave. So masters and their families clung to slaves out of affection and need, and surely some slaves, though all detested servitude, came to have some affection for their masters and their families.[19]

Slave women were not as numerous as slave men. The colony's sex ratio widened as slave imports rose during the 1730s, peaking at about 170 men to every 100 women. The natural growth rate (the ratio of children born to slaves who died) turned negative in this decade—the enormous growth of the slave population propelled entirely by imports. This made women far more valuable to the men within the slave community than the women, old hands or newcomers, were to the masters. But unsavory and

19. Terrence W. Epperson, "'A Separate House for the Christian Slaves, One for the Negro Slaves': The Archeology of Race and Identity in Late Seventeenth-Century Virginia," in *Race and the Archeology of Identity*, ed. Charles E. Orser Jr. (Salt Lake City: University of Utah Press, 2001), 54–67; Coclanis, *Shadow of a Dream*, 111; Andrea N. Williams, Introduction, "Narrative of the Life of Moses Grandy," in *North Carolina Slave Narratives*, ed. William L. Andrews et al. (Chapel Hill: University of North Carolina Press, 2003), 141; Morgan, *Slave Counterpoint*, 113, 378, 382.

unwarranted sexual innuendo demeaned slave women even as it seemed to admire them. The *South-Carolina Gazette* snidely applauded "African ladies…of strong robust constitution…not easily jaded out" by hours of lovemaking.[20]

A few female slaves, often pre-teens or older women, might serve within the plantation household as cooks, maids, laundresses, and nannies, but most worked in the fields. Before the introduction of steam-driven rice mills, slaves had to pound the harvested plants. Women (and men) did benefit from one peculiarity of rice cultivation. Under the so-called task system, when the slave's allotted task for the day was done, the slave's time belonged to the slave. Elsewhere in the British Empire, slaves worked in gangs from sunup to sundown, the only concession to the slave's physical condition was placement on the second or third gang, where working conditions were less onerous.[21]

Despite the respite from labor afforded slaves by the task system, the slave had no real privacy, for the slave was the master's chattel (a personal belonging), and property has no privacy. The dreaded patrols created by law in the southern colonies might enter slave dwellings whenever the patrollers wished. The patrols tried to turn night into day, carrying lanterns with them as they traversed the land, and insisted that slaves make light in their homes to aid the patrollers' investigations.[22]

20. Morgan, *Slave Counterpoint*, 81–83; *South-Carolina Gazette* essay, 1736, quoted in *Ar'n't I a Woman: Female Slaves in the Plantation South*, by Deborah Gray White (New York: Norton, 1985), 30.

21. Morgan, *Slave Counterpoint*, 179–182.

22. Sally E. Hadden, *Slave Patrols: Law and Violence in Virginia and the Carolinas* (Cambridge, Mass.: Harvard University Press, 2001), 107.

But slaves responded as resourcefully to the patrols as they did to their masters' commands. Just as slaves became inarticulate or deferential to divert their masters' anger, so they became invisible to avoid the patrols. Darkness was their ally. Men and women made regular trips at night to visit other slaves. In 1688 Governor Francis Nicholson of Maryland was struck by the distance slaves traveled at night "to go and see another tho' at 30 or 40 miles distance." Sometimes the night travelers walked alone, but Nicholson met six or seven at a time during the holidays.[23]

Some slaves turned to African magic ways to cloak themselves as they roamed the countryside at night. There was a healthy trade in charms and potions for a variety of purposes, and conjurors in the quarters offered roots, herbs, and potions to induce temporary invisibility. Not content with magic, wily slaves laid trip wires across roads to foil the patrols and detoured through swamps, or rubbed manure or turpentine on themselves to put tracking dogs off the scent. Slaves set sentries to warn that the patrols were near.[24]

Another form of invisibility was running away. Slavery was first and foremost a labor system, and the runaway could not contribute his or her labor to the owners' or lessees' enterprise. Running away was so common that the law developed a category for the habitual runaway—the "redhibitory slave." Such slaves were not to be sold without a warning to the buyer, and buyers

23. Nicholson, quoted in Sobel, *World They Made Together*, 33.
24. Hadden, *Slave Patrols*, 108–109, 116–117, 132.

could seek rescission of the sale if the slave ran away from the new owner.[25]

Most slaves did not run far. Slave runaways often hid in plain sight. Many of the advertisements about runaways noted that the slave was "well known in the area." The "molatto named Franke…is known by most people in Charles Town, and without doubt harbored by some free Negroes or slaves." She had probably crossed paths with Minos, "now supposed to be lurking in or about the town." This meant that the slave had family or friends or countrymen nearby. South Carolina law forbade slaves and free blacks from "harboring or concealing" a runaway, which implies that many runaways were concealed and harbored in precisely this fashion. On plantations, runaway slaves used the outbuildings as hideouts. Landon's Carter's slave Simon was a master of disappearing when work was hardest. He merely lived with nearby slave kin. Runaways ran into one another, spreading gossip from one plantation to another, or making plans for more serious crimes.[26]

25. James Sidbury, *Ploughshares into Swords: Race, Rebellion, and Identity in Gabriel's Virginia, 1730–1810* (Cambridge: Cambridge University Press, 1997), 24; Ariela J. Gross, *Double Character: Slavery and Mastery in the Antebellum Southern Courtroom* (Princeton: Princeton University Press, 2000), 34; and, generally, Ira Berlin and Philip D. Morgan, eds., *Cultivation and Culture: Labor and the Shaping of Slave Life in the Americas* (Charlottesville: University of Virginia Press, 1993).

26. Windley, *Runaway Slave Advertisements*, 3:9–10; Act of 1740, in *Public Laws….of South Carolina*, comp. John F. Grimké, 1:170; Isaac, *Transformation of Virginia*, 335–341; Winthrop D. Jordan, *Tumult and Silence at Second Creek: An Inquiry into a Civil War Slave Conspiracy*, rev. ed. (Baton Rouge: Louisiana State University Press, 1995), 124.

There was an epidemic of running away in the closing years of the decade, corresponding to the influx of slave imports because most runaways were newcomers. The historian Sally Hadden reports that "every rumor about possible freedom seemed to reach the remotest slave cabin." The incentive to decamp increased as rumors spread of an impending war with Spain. Spanish Florida lay about two hundred miles from Charles Town, and Spain's imperial government had ordered Florida to welcome runaway slaves from South Carolina, arm them, and allow them the freedom of the colony. There is some evidence that the Spanish authorities in the colony were actively inciting slave unrest. Governor Manuel Montiano, who arrived in the colony in 1737, had that project high on his agenda. As news of deteriorating relations between Britain and Spain became a major topic of conversation among the whites, house slaves listened carefully and passed the news to field hands in the quarters. For the whites, Spanish Florida was a peril. For the slaves, it was a haven—distant but envisioned as just over the horizon. Undoubtedly some knew about the runaway slave town of Mose, in Spanish Florida, where men of color were free to carry arms and had their own fort. Some slaves got no farther than nearby marshes and inland scrub; some made it to all the way to Florida. In 1738 seventy slaves fled the colony and reached St. Augustine, Florida, 278 miles from Charles Town.[27]

27. Hadden, *Slave Patrols*, 152, 153; Wood, *Black Majority*, 238–267; Morgan, *Slave Counterpoint*, 450. On Mose, see Jane Landers, "Garcia Real de Santa Teresa de Mose: A Free Black Town in Spanish Colonial Florida," *American Historical Review* 95 (1990), 9–30; on Spanish policy, "Dispatches of Spanish Officials Bearing on the Free Negro Settlement of Garcia Real de Santa Teresa de Mose," *Journal of Negro History* 9 (1924), 144–195.

Owners responded to the rash of runaways by marking their slaves, as they did their cattle and swine. Benjamin Godin had taken the precaution of branding his new Angolans with the initials "BG" on their chests, but Harry, Cyrus, and Chatham had taken off nonetheless. They joined Sam and Gambia in flight from his plantation. In the spring of 1738, Thomas Wright lost Paul, who in his year's stay in the colony had learned no English; Charles, an elderly man with the initials "TW" branded on his shoulder: and two new arrivals, though they had already been branded with the owner's initials on their shoulders. By the summer, Wright had lost five more men, two in Charles Town, two from his Silk-Hope plantation, and one "near Stono Church." The last, "a Negro boy named Bellfast, pretty tall, had on a blue coast, the sleeves turned up with black." Bellfast had with him one of Wright's mounts, a "young grey horse, branded upon the buttock," unlike Bellfast, who was seared with a "TW" on the shoulder.[28]

Recaptured slaves would be punished—most often, and most visibly, by a whipping. It not only left marks on the body and the hearts of slaves but was the centerpiece in a public ritual whose impact on other slaves derived in large measure from its visibility. Though whipping might not be an everyday occurrence, still the spectacle of the public whipping carried a different tenor than the private chastisement of a servant or a child. The master required other slaves to witness the punishment of one of their number— "to let them know" who had the power.[29]

28. Windley, *Runaway Slave Advertisements*, 3:31–34.
29. Stephen Pembroke, a runaway slave, quoted in the *New York Tribune*, July 18, 1854, reprinted in *Slave Testimony: Two Centuries of Letters, Speeches,*

The message was received. The former slave Margaret Hughes recalled, "Once I saw my poor old daddy in chains, they chained his feet together, and his hands too, and carry him off to whip him." Nearly seventy-five years after the event, the image was still fresh in her mind. Jerry Hill similarly recalled how the whites reacted to "various slaves whipped that day for various things, and there were several men around standing and watching...one laughed." The impact of whipping outlasted the pain and shame: the slave with many visible marks on his or her back was branded a malcontent, malingerer, or worse.[30]

Whites did not have slaves on their minds all the time, and slaves did not always plot resistance to slavery. Sometimes the meetings of strangers were cordial, or at least amicable. John Wesley, an Anglican minister and later the founder of Methodism, was traveling for the Society for the Propagation of the Gospel in Foreign Parts from Georgia's capital of Savannah to Charles Town in the winter of 1737. Unable to return to Georgia by ship because of a storm, Wesley was lent a horse by the minister at Pon Pon Chapel, in St. Bartholomew's Parish, Colleton, and the English missionary traveled back to Savannah on the Pon Pon

---

Interviews, and Autobiographies, ed. John W. Blassingame (Baton Rouge: Louisiana State University Press, 1977), 139. Whipping was the most common form of severe corporal punishment, Robert Olwell, *Masters, Slaves, and Subjects: The Culture of Power in the South Carolina Low Country, 1740–1790* (Baltimore: Johns Hopkins University Press, 1998), 148.

30. George P. Rawick, ed., *The American Slave, Volume 2: South Carolina Narratives* (Westport, Conn.: Greenwood, 1972), 328, 289; Gross, *Double Character*, 130.

road. He spent nights at obliging planters' homes and was guided by slaves from one home to the next.

Wesley found that the slaves went to church but did not understand the preaching. Intrigued, he tried to report Christ's message to the slaves. He did not use the methods that the Jesuits and Recollects used in French Canada, teaching by drawing pictures and by combining Christianity with the converts' traditions, but he did simplify the gospels. "There is something in you that will not turn to dust," he told his host's young black servant, "and this is what they call your soul." One could not see it, but God had implanted it there. "It is He that made you and me, and all men and women, and all beasts and birds and all the world. It is He that makes the sun shine and the rain fall and corn and fruits to grow out of the ground. It makes it all for us." In a very short version of the catechism, he asked the rapt young woman, "But why do you think He made us? What did he make you and me for?" She replied, "I can't tell." Wesley had the answer, one of comfort and aspiration: "He made you to live with himself above the sky. And so you will, in a little time, if you are good....No one will beat or hurt you there."

He preached the same message twice at the Pon Pon chapel, confident that those who heard and understood the message— planters and their bondmen and women, would find true peace with one another. "Perhaps one of the easiest and shortest ways to instruct the American Negroes in Christianity," he surmised, "would be to find out some of the most serious of the planters. Then, having enquired of them, which of their slaves were best inclined and understood English, to go to them from plantation to plantation, and staying as long as appeared necessary in each."

It did not happen that way, and Wesley soon returned to his own congregation in Savannah.[31]

Hundreds of slaves turned out to hear the Anglican missionary George Whitefield preach in Georgia and South Carolina in 1738. They may or may not have understood the intricacies of Christian theology, but they understood the underlying message—in Jesus there was salvation, if not in this world, in the next. Whitefield was a galvanizing preacher, his voice carrying great distances, and his message deeply touching the emotions of his auditory. He preached in fields and churches to overflowing crowds. Slaves coming back from these events must have felt a spirituality that, if it did not amount to conversion, certainly changed how they saw their world. A few South Carolina planters even sponsored "biracial" evangelical meetings. However, historians still debate the extent to which the enslaved read Christianity in terms of African religious beliefs.[32]

31. John Wesley, *The Journal of the Reverend John Wesley* (London: Kershaw, 1827), 1:45–46. But some of the slaves prayed Christian prayers in Kikongo, a fact that Wesley, who did not much care for Catholicism, either ignored or did not know. Ira Berlin, "From Creole to African," in *How Did American Slavery Begin?* ed. Edward Countryman (New York: Macmillan, 1999), 41.

32. Jon F. Sensbach, *Rebecca's Revival: Creating Black Christianity in the Atlantic World* (Cambridge, Mass.: Harvard University Press, 2006), 138; William F. Politzer, *The Gullah People and the African Heritage* (Athens: University of Georgia Press, 2005), 149–151. Historians have likened Whitefield's preaching to a kind of public performance. See, e.g., Harry S. Stout, *The Divine Dramatist: George Whitefield and the Rise of Modern Evangelism* (Grand Rapids: W. B. Eerdmans, 1991); Frank Lambert, *"Pedlar in Divinity": George Whitefield and the Transatlantic Revivals, 1737–1770* (Princeton: Princeton University Press, 1994).

But every encounter between groups of enslaved men and free whites raised the possibility of conflict. The naturalist William Bartram, traveling in rural South Carolina in the 1770s, recorded one such meeting where he "observed a number of persons coming up ahead, whom [he] soon perceived to be a party of Negroes." He wrote, "I had every reason to dread the consequence, for this being a desolate place, I was by this time several miles from any house or plantation, and had reason to apprehend this a predatory band of Negroes....I was alone, unarmed, and my horse tired; thus situated in every way in their power. I had no alternative but to be resigned and meet them....Thus prepared, when we drew near to each other, I mounted and rode briskly up, and though armed with clubs, axes and hoes, they opened to right and left, and let me pass peaceably."[33] The Negroes were a work party of slaves, some of the thousands who ditched and weeded, bringing land under the cultivation of the rice planters. Such work gangs were as familiar in the landscape as the swamps and savannahs, the mangrove copses and the marsh grass seas that fringed the South Carolina colony.

❧

The experiences of the slaves who came to the store teach lessons about slavery quite different from the ones that a literal reading of the laws might suggest. Slaves were not objects, they were people, and highly mobile ones at that. They did not remain on the plantations but moved over the land and the waterways. They hunted and fished on their days of rest, visited with friends

33. William Bartram, *The Travels of William Bartram* [1791], ed. Mark Van Doren (New York: Macy-Masius, 1928), 373.

and relatives on neighboring plantations, or simply found quiet places far from the fields. Slave boatmen carrying passengers or cargo and slave fishermen were more mobile than some of their masters. In Charles Town, where slaves loaded and unloaded ships, drove carts, sold and bought for their masters (and themselves), they behaved as if free. They dressed in bright colors in costumes of their own design, worshiped in churches, and carried themselves proudly. As Robert Olwell has written of the slaves "if possession were ever indeed nine-tenths of the law, slaves may well have had a case for claiming the streets as their own."[34]

Nor did the rural landscape belong to its legal owners. If having the land beneath one's feet was a kind of possession, South Carolina belonged to its slaves. Mobility conferred a certain kind of autonomy. The historian S. Max Edelson states that "as plantations stretched out across the land, slave quarters tended to migrate away from this seat of white scrutiny. Settled near the fields in which they worked, slaves might be left to their own devices for much of the time provided they completed their assigned tasks." Slave quarters became little communities, in many ways autonomous and self-defining. In the quarters, some slaves became important figures—men and women to whom other men and women looked for guidance. In the quarters, there was space and time for a little garden, for play, for courting, for childcare, for telling stories, for going off to hunt or fish, or, perhaps, for plotting rebellion. Out of sight of the planter did not mean out of mind, but the very process

34. Olwell, *Masters, Slaves, and Subjects*, 20.

by which slavery expanded stretched the bonds of discipline to near the breaking point.[35]

There surely was a tipping point, however, a time when so many new slaves on the land would overburden the frail system of control. Even newcomers such as the French Huguenots Gabriel Manigault in the Beaufort District at the southern end of the colony and Daniel Huger, whose plantation was in Berkeley County, north and east of Charles Town, could count hundreds of slaves on their plantations. The increased importation of Africans placed an almost intolerable burden on everyone, free and slave. As the number of slaves skyrocketed in the 1720s and 1730s, mortality rates began to spike. The total number of slaves grew 300 percent, but slaves reckoned that old comrades and new friends would die before they could start families. Something had to give, and on the night of September 8, 1739, it did.[36]

35. S. Max Edelson, *Plantation Enterprise in Colonial South Carolina* (Cambridge, Mass.: Harvard University Press, 2006), 115; Anthony E. Kaye, *Joining Places: Slave Neighborhoods in the Old South* (Chapel Hill: University of North Carolina Press, 2007), 8–9, 119–151.

36. Weir, *Colonial South Carolina*, 187; Jon Butler, *The Huguenots in America: A Refugee People in a New World Society* (Cambridge, Mass.: Harvard University Press, 1983), 122.

· *Three* ·

TERROR IN THE NIGHT

❦

ON FEBRUARY 21, 1739, WILLIAM DRAYTON OF ST. JOHNS Colleton reported to the assembly of the colony a project for digging passages into the North Branch of the Stono River. Such trenches, or drains, were the forerunners of the modern storm sewer. They were fifteen feet to twenty feet wide and six feet in depth. After storms, freshets from the Stono and other rivers made roads impassable; carried debris into the rivers themselves, making them impassable; and generally wreaked havoc with the transportation of goods and services. The drains did double duty leaching the waters out of swamps, leaving the land dry enough for cultivation. Some drains remain and are little canals that nature lovers traverse in kayaks.

The planter Thomas Elliott of Colleton carried the bill, which, after amendment, was titled "a bill to cut and sink drains and passages on the North Branch of the Stono River," up to the council, the upper house of the legislature. But the bill met resistance. Planters such as John Williams and Ann Drayton objected to cuts and drains on their land. So insistent were they that the lower house appointed "counsel learned in the law" to hear and resolve the dispute.[1]

David Hext led the team of mediators, and Solomon-like they agreed that the cuts were to go in Horse Savannah, Jack's Savannah, and Long Savannah, undeveloped lands, and that the commissioners were to ensure that "the several inhabitants within the said district equally and proportionally" benefited "according to the quantity of overlown [covered over with water] land each person [was] possessed of." Horse Savannah still exists, at the upper edge of Wallace Creek. It is still swampland, but now eyed by estate developers (the road through it is being widened). In 1739 the cuts were a public improvement, and private owners had to accept some small detriment to their own holdings. The modern concept of "eminent domain" works the same way, when a homeowner surrenders frontage for new sidewalks or storm drains. It was a major public works project, the only one the legislature considered for the coming summer.[2]

The three savannahs covered many thousands of acres just north of the Stono. Like carrying out the road-repair projects, cutting drains was hard work, but unlike the roadwork, digging ditches in

1. Ralph Izard's petition to the Commons House, February 21, 1739, *Journal of the Commons House of Assembly, November 10, 1736–June 7, 1739*, 632, 647–648; objections to the bill appeared on March 20, 1739, pp. 674, 678. The width and depth of cuts varied; see, e.g., Sessions Laws, May 1740, *Acts Passed by the General Assembly of South-Carolina, May 10, 1740–July 10, 1742* (Charles Town, S.C.: Peter Timothy, 1742), 131–136.

2. April 6, 1739, *Journal of the Commons House of Assembly, November 10, 1736–June 7, 1739*, pp. 691–692.

wetlands was dangerous. Bending over shovels and mattocks in the snake- and insect-infested waters, the diggers were exposed to the elements, disease, and exhaustion. The summer's heat would create terrible thirst, but the brackish water at the diggers' feet was filled with deadly bacteria, parasites, and waste. Overseers or the commissioners themselves were to be present, but, as later legislation revealed, they were often negligent in this regard.[3]

South Carolina law gave to the parish commissioners the power to set every and any slave aged sixteen to sixty to work on the public roads and waterways. The slaves were to come from the surrounding plantations. Planters who did not provide slaves were to be fined ten pounds colony money. For masters whose slaves did not appear on an appointed day, the fine was 12 shillings 6 pence. The legislators, planters themselves, knew that planters did not send their best or most valued slaves to this backbreaking task.[4]

3. The "Negro Act," Sessions Laws, 1740, was filled with admonitions to masters, whites who dealt with slaves, anyone who bought from or sold to slaves, and all officials to watch slaves carefully. For absent overseers, Sally E. Hadden, *Slave Patrols: Law and Violence in Virginia and the Carolinas* (Cambridge, Mass.: Harvard University Press, 2001), 81; Philip Morgan, *Slave Counterpoint: Black Culture in the Eighteenth-Century Chesapeake and Low Country* (Chapel Hill: University of North Carolina Press, 1998), 330–336.

4. For example, on the Stono River, see Act of 1754, in *Public Laws of…South Carolina*, comp. Grimké, 1:229–230; Statute of 1740, in *Public Laws of…South Carolina*, comp. Grimké, 1:168. These statutes, while passed after Stono, merely codified long-standing usages. Morgan, *Slave Counterpoint*, 186, 202. The task system prevalent in South Carolina gave slaves time to themselves when their assigned tasks for the day or week were done. This did not apply to labor on river gangs, however, or road crews.

Slaves in the Low Country worked on the task system. When a task was done, their time was their own—within limits. Slavery afforded no privacy, but the task system was a boon of sorts to the slaves to make space for gardens and entertainment. The law also provided that slaves were not to be worked on the Sabbath. But the law also gave to the commissioners of roads (and drains) the authority to overrule that provision. The savannah drains had to be completed before the fall storms, and with the project late getting underway (while its opponents bargained with its proponents in the legislature), time was of the essence. The slaves of the drain crew, perhaps as many as two dozen, surely knew that long, hard, and unrelieved labor stretched before them.[5]

5. "An Act to Impower the Several Commissioners of the High-roads...and Cleaning of Water Passages," September 15, 1721, *Earliest Printed Laws of South Carolina, 1692–1734*, ed. John D. Cushing, 1:357–366. Most of the accounts of the rebellion assert that some of the rebels came from a "road crew." The origin of this is a comment in an 1770 report to his English superiors by Lieutenant Governor William Bull Jr., son of the acting lieutenant governor William Bull. Bull's surmise is discussed in the headnote to his report, in Mark M. Smith, ed., *Stono: Documenting and Interpreting a Southern Slave Revolt* (Columbia: University of South Carolina Press, 2005), 30, and H. Roy Merrens, ed., *The Colonial South Carolina Scene: Contemporary Views, 1697–1774* (Columbia: University of South Carolina Press, 1977), 260. The reference to a road crew, as opposed to a drainage crew, was likely a natural mistake, the younger Bull relying on the memory of what his father had told him, as no provision was made for public-works funding for roads in the area at that time. There was, however, funding for the drainage of the Horse Savannah, next door (so to speak) to the Stono crossing where the violence erupted. The argument that a work crew would become the core of the rebels is found in Michael Mullin, *Africa in America: Slave Acculturalization and Resistance in the American South, 1736–1831* (Urbana: University of Illinois Press, 1992), 43; *Encyclopedia*

Many on the crew must have been new to the colony, not the most trusted and valued of slaves. Some, perhaps most, of the newcomers came from the Kongo region of Southwest Africa. These newcomers did not accede to their bondage gracefully. In the 1730s nearly 80 percent (72 men and women) of the runaways reported in the newspaper were newcomers from Angola or Kongo. Though later, somewhat romantically, these Kongolese were reputed to be "gentle with an affectionate nature" and "faithful to a trust," in fact almost all were soldiers defeated in civil wars and enslaved. Some were Catholics, having been converted by Portuguese missionaries in Africa. If they had heard of the Florida authorities promising freedom, they would have taken the offer seriously. Though they did not know the trails as well as the locally born slaves, they knew how to orient themselves (a skill that all infantry needed to master) and could follow the sun and the stars to freedom.[6]

---

of World Slavery (New York: Macmillan, 1998), 881, and Peter Charles Hoffer, *Sensory Worlds in Early America* (Baltimore: Johns Hopkins University Press, 2003), 152. It is an inference: the only body of men large enough to become the core of the rebels and yet whose absence from their plantations would not be noticed would be a work crew. For the two dozen field workers who usually composed a work crew, I have relied upon paintings and pictures of South Carolina field workers. See, e.g., the depictions in *South Carolina Then and Now* (Columbia: South Carolina Department of Archives and History, 2001); John Michael Vlach, *The Planter's Prospect: Privilege and Slavery in Plantation Paintings* (Chapel Hill: University of North Carolina Press, 2001); and Angela Mack, ed., *The Landscape of Slavery: the Plantation in American Art* (Columbia: University of South Carolina Press, 2008).

6. Dubose Heyward, "The Negro in the Low Country," in *The Carolina Low-Country* (New York: Macmillan, 1934), 173; John Thornton, "The African Dimensions of the Stono Rebellion," *American Historical*

Imagine, then, sundown, September 8. Most of the whites and blacks in the colony have finished their labors and look forward to the day of rest to come, but the drain crew bristle with discontent. There would be no day of rest for them tomorrow, even though it was the Sabbath. For the ditch crew could not rest until the ditches were cut. At dusk the mosquitoes swarmed, the heat of the slaves' bodies drawing clouds of the pests. The men remembered with a kind of desperate longing homes far away, missing and loved kinfolk and wives. Even the Catholic converts among them believed that their spirits could never be one with their ancestors', not until they could journey back to their African homes.

Under normal circumstances the men should have returned to the slave quarters on their plantations, but the overseer had left before nightfall, and the diggers were left to their own devices and desires. Bone tired, thirsty, and hungry, they griped in the way that manual laborers do at the end of the workday. There was no plan to raise the countryside in rebellion, no grand scheme

---

Review 96 (October 1991), 1103; David C. Littlefield, *Rice and Slaves: Ethnicity and the Slave Trade in Colonial South Carolina* (Baton Rouge: Louisiana State University Press, 1981), tables at 121, 122, 126. Mark Smith, "Remembering Mary, Shaping Revolt: Reconsidering the Stono Rebellion," *Journal of Southern History* 67 (2001), 513–534, argues that "the Kongolese knew their Catholic calendar." At the same time, they were syncretists; that is, they fused Christianity with African forms and ideas of worship. But to imply that all the Kongolese in South Carolina were Catholic, or that their Catholicism was of a sort that determined their motives, feelings, and plans, is something of a reach. Joseph Miller, *Way of Death: Merchant Capitalism and the Angolan Slave Trade, 1730–1830* (Madison: University of Wisconsin Press, 1996), 246, describes "colonials of Angolan birth, with a veneer of Portuguese Catholicism, dress and language overlaid on local non-Catholic religious beliefs."

to undo slavery, no plot to run riot. The grumbling simply got worse, gaining focus and momentum.

Some among the crew reminded the others of the gossip they had overheard at the market fairs held in the countryside, or from their overseers or masters' conversations: There was a war coming, a war with Spain, and the masters were worried about the security of the colony. For the crew, the talk of war bore a different aspect. It might work to their advantage. The dangers that the war posed to South Carolina's long, exposed coastline might provide an opportunity to escape from the colony. Others in the crew had seen the panicky migration out of the Low Country of white families fleeing from the smallpox epidemic. Each bit of information, like spices thrown into a stew pot, gave new flavor to the conversation. Put this information together with the whispers of Spain's policy of freeing runaway English colonial slaves, and the prospects for a general uprising became more attractive.[7]

In hindsight, both the lieutenant governor of South Carolina, William Bull, and the governor general of neighboring Georgia, James Oglethorpe, thought that the rumors of war were potent goads to all slaves to plot resistance. On October 17, 1739, Bull wrote to his English masters, warning of "the desertion of our Negroes, who are encouraged to it by a certain proclamation published by the King of Spain's order at St. Augustine declaring freedom to all Negroes who should desert thither from the

7. This is precisely the line of thought of the slave rebels in New York City, in 1741. Peter Charles Hoffer, *The Great New York Conspiracy of 1741: Slavery, Crime, and Colonial Law* (Lawrence: University Press of Kansas, 2003), 73.

British colonies, since which several parties have deserted and are there openly received and protected." The word had spread, and "many other attempts of others" had been "discovered and prevented."[8]

Oglethorpe had more information at his disposal. "There was a proclamation published at [St.] Augustine in which the king of Spain (then at peace with Great Britain) promised protection and freedom to all Negroes slaves that would resort thither." The baneful consequences were immediate, according to Oglethorpe: "Certain Negroes belonging to Captain Davis escaped to Augustine, and were received there. They were demanded by General Oglethorpe," but the Spanish governor showed Oglethorpe's emissary the proclamation. Nothing could be done. But "of this other Negroes having notice, as it is believed, from the Spanish emissaries, four or five [slaves] who were cattle hunters, and knew the woods" made for Augustine. They stole their master's horses, "wounded his son and killed another man." The rangers were not able to catch the runaways, and though they passed by Ebenezer, the Salzburgers did nothing to impede their progress to Augustine. Indians paid to chase them were able to kill one, but the rest "were received there [in St. Augustine] with great honors, one of them had a commission given to him, and a coat faced with velvet."[9]

8. William Bull to the Board of Trade, October 5, 1739, C.O. [Colonial Office] papers 1730–1746, 5/388, copy in South Carolina Department of Archives and History [SCDAH], Columbia, S.C., Records in the British Public Record Office Pertaining to South Carolina, 1711–1782, vol. 20, 179–180.

9. "An Account of the Negroe Insurrection in South Carolina," *Colonial Records of the State of Georgia*, ed. Allen D. Candler, William L. Northern, and Lucian L. Knight (Atlanta: Byrd, 1913), vol. 22 (part 2): 232–236.

If the coming war (and it did in fact come) with Spain made Spanish Florida an attractive destination for slaves, the rumors should have turned the drain crew's thoughts to flight, not fighting. Running away was a kind of passive resistance—an "insubordination" defying the domination/subordination relationship at the heart of slave discipline. Some voices in the crew were raised in support of desertion: Join the runaways, make for Florida, run the back ways; stay away from the patrols, the rangers, the Indians hired to hunt down runaways; and abandon friends and family. Newcomers were the most likely to run. Why not now?[10]

Most group runaways were composed of work-group members. They simply took off together. On the other hand, most slave runaways did not abscond or travel in groups. They fled alone or with a companion. The risk of "betrayal, detection, and capture," based in part on a change of heart by one of the group or by the disturbance a group made, deterred runaways from banding together.[11]

10. Allan Kulikoff, *Tobacco and Slaves: The Development of Southern Cultures in the Chesapeake, 1680–1800* (Chapel Hill: University of North Carolina Press, 1986), 328.

11. Michael P. Johnson, "Runaway Slaves and Slave Communities in South Carolina, 1799 to 1830," *William and Mary Quarterly*, 3rd ser., 38 (July 1981), 420, 422. My use of these data is an example of "upstreaming," using sources from a later time to throw light on events that occurred earlier. This is a very common technique in the study of Native Americans; for example, see Daniel Richter, *Facing East from Indian Country: A Native History of Early America* (Cambridge, Mass.: Harvard University Press, 2001), 14–15. In upstreaming, one has to assume that the later motives and behaviors of slaves reflected a continuation of motives and behaviors of slaves in earlier times. On the later slaves' thinking, see Charles Joyner, *Down by the Riverside: A South Carolina Slave Community* (Urbana: University of Illinois Press, 1984), 233.

Others in the drainage crew objected to a mass breakout. So large a group would not be able to get out of South Carolina, cross the Savannah River, evade the Georgia rangers on the way through that colony, and reach the border with Florida (itself a matter of dispute between the British and the Spanish empires, and hence likely to be occupied by troops). The trip would require speed, stealth, and determination. If they decided to undertake the enterprise, they must begin immediately, run through the night and into the next day. But they were already dead tired, and they deserved a little rest and relaxation, not more, and more dangerous, exertion.

Then, too, running, especially at night, requires enough light to see the way. South Carolina law required that Charles Town slaves abroad at night on legitimate business carry lanterns (along with passes from their masters). Slaves in the quarters might have access to lanterns (though at this time even the cheapest of them were a luxury item), but carrying a lit one down the road at night was a sure way to attract the attention of the patrol. Indeed, patrols carried lanterns themselves. A full moon on a clear night, by contrast, could show the way to freedom, but on the night of September 8, 1739, the moon was in its first quarter. It would not be full until September 17.[12]

Evidently the voices in favor of seeking out a place to put up their heels and "frolick" won out for a time over the angrier voices. Hutchenson's store, across the Stono Bridge from the work site, was the nearest source of liquid refreshment and victuals. It was too late for the store to be open for business, and in any case the

---

12. *South-Carolina Gazette*, March 19, 1737; Arthur H. Hayward, *Colonial Lighting* (Boston: Little, Brown, 1927), 55; on the phases of the moon that night, see eclipse.gsfc.nasa.gov/phase/phases1701.html.

crew had no intention of purchasing the food and drink. So the men turned their attention and their feet to the bridge over the Stono and Hutchenson's stock.

Or perhaps the foregoing imaginative reconstruction of events may be wrong. The members of the drain crew may have simply gone back to their plantations and taken no part in the mayhem in the hours that followed. A different aggregation of Angolan newcomers may have been plotting a general rebellion and chosen this night to execute their plan. According to this account—the conventional narrative of the Stono rebellion—the rebels broke into Hutchenson's in order to obtain firearms, and then set the countryside aflame. The problem with this account is that a plot involving any large number of slaves would almost certainly be revealed to the masters before it could effect itself. The larger the plan, the greater the number of slaves who knew about it, and a disaffected plotter or a slave seeking to curry favor with his master, or a loyal slave who overheard the plotters, always informed on them. If the plotters were Angolans, then non-Angolans would resent the newcomers' assumption of leadership. There was little class solidarity among the slaves.[13]

Let us pause for a moment, leaving the tired men as they made their way to Hutchenson's. In the coming hours, it is most likely

13. The best short summary of the conventional story are the reprinted selections from Peter Wood and others in Smith, *Stono*, 59–124. On the likelihood that slaves would reveal plots, see, for example, the slave who denounced an alleged plot in 1740, outside of Charleston, in Olwell, *Masters, Slaves, and Subjects*, 27; the slaves who revealed a plot in Camden, S.C., some years later, in Lacy K. Ford, *Deliver Us from Evil: The Slavery Question in the Old South* (New York: Oxford University Press, 2009), 174–175; or the slave who almost casually let on that Denmark Vesey and his congregants were planning an uprising in 1820, ibid., 206 and after. A slave informant

that some of these men, joined by other slaves, would kill white men and women and burn their homes. They would become a rebel band, marching down King's Highway, calling out "Liberty!" to other slaves to join their uprising. In this, they would become part of a far larger story of violent resistance to the inherent violence of slavery. But historians should not homogenize all slave actors and motives, nor telescope the long history of slavery into a single event, nor make heroic or homicidal what was not. Nor should we assume that actions are all planned and responses to the unforeseen are all programmed. There is in human action an irony that makes a hash of all our plans. True enough, every slave dreamed of freedom and many no doubt plotted their way to an imagined liberty, but rarely did any of these plots lead to action.[14]

Perhaps the difficulty in comprehending causes and effects at this stage of the evening's events lies in the word "rebellion" itself. Did it have to have an ideology behind it, an intellectual rationale, or could it be a simple act? Did it have to portend a general rising, like the Irish rebellion of the early twentieth century, or could it consist of the actions of only a few people? When

---

revealed Gabriel's rebellion in Richmond, in 1800: Douglas R. Egerton, *Gabriel's Rebellion: The Virginia Slave Conspiracies of 1800–1802* (Chapel Hill: University of North Carolina Press, 1993), 69–73. The exception, admittedly a very important one, was Nat Turner's murder spree in 1831.

14. Historians agree that the actual number of slave rebellions in the North American colonies, indeed during the entire course of slavery in the mainland colonies and in the United States was remarkably small, given the huge number of slaves and the vast slave territories. Betty Wood, *Slavery in Colonial America* (Lanham, Md.: Rowman and Littlefield, 2005), 62–64; Winthrop D. Jordan, *White over Black: American Attitudes toward the Negro, 1550–1812* (Chapel Hill: University of North Carolina Press, 1968), 113.

did individual acts of violence become a rebellion and assailants become rebels? Historians must reduce real actions in the past to words. Rebellion is thus as much our choice of terminology as something in itself that we discover.[15]

15. Historians read the story of the rebellion backward from the violence of September 9 to the assumption of a ripening plot in preceding days. All of the modern accounts of the twenty-four hours of violence also write backward; that is, they too begin by terming the events of the next day "an insurrection" and then read motive and action back into the early evening from that depiction. As Edward Pearson wrote, "The tocsin of rebellion rang in early hours of Sunday morning on 9 September as rebellious slaves assembled outside Hutchenson's store under Jemmy's leadership." Jemmy was a name supplied in 1739 to James Oglethorpe, governor general of neighboring Georgia. Jemmy was supposedly a rebel, a planner, and a plotter, who had chosen Sunday morning because the masters would be at church. Led by this archetypal Jemmy (the name simply standing for all slave rebel leaders) or by Cato (the name supplied by a later historian), the rebels at Stono simply inverted the power relationship, making themselves masters for a time of their own fates, along with that of all the whites who stood in their path to freedom. Walter Rucker classed the day as "the most disturbing colonial era revolt in North America," while Peter Wood termed the events "a rebellion...put into immediate execution without hesitancy or betrayal" and with "an air of particular confidence." Edward Pearson, "'Countryside Full of Flames': A Reconsideration of the Stono Rebellion and Slaves Rebelliousness in the Early Eighteenth-Century South Carolina Lowcountry," *Slavery and Abolition* 17 (August 1996), 37–38; Walter C. Rucker, *The River Flows On: Black Resistance, Culture, and Identity Formation in Early America* (Baton Rouge: Louisiana State University Press, 2006), 100; Peter Wood, *Black Majority: Negroes in Colonial South Carolina through the Stono Rebellion* (New York: Norton, 1973), 314. In passing, one wonders in what language the Angolans called out "liberty," it being an English word. The source of the information was an English speaker, and he probably did not know the Bantu for liberty, no more than the Angolans knew the English word. An interesting puzzle raised nicely by Justin Pope in a conversation with the author.

Perhaps we need to turn the question on its head and ask why slaves who suffered so much from the anger of cruel masters did not rebel more often. Despite the "spectacular nature of black suffering" under slavery, Stono was in fact the only major uprising in the history of British North America. The relative paucity of slave uprisings has led scholars to speculate about future rebels' motives. Scholars agree that the penalties for a failed rebellion were so severe that they would have caused the boldest would-be rebel to pause. But not all the slaves at Stono had seen a failed rebellion, and many did not know firsthand what would happen to suspected rebels (though surely they could guess). Although the solidarity of the whites and the closeness of supervision of slaves on the plantation usually deterred would-be rebels among longtime slaves, the many newcomers assigned to the drainage crew might not have anticipated the strength of white solidarity, in particular the fury with which the entire white population would come out against them.[16]

If my reconstruction of the evening's beginning is plausible, at least for the motives of some of the enslaved, the revolt was not triggered by the obtrusive supervision of whites in general or by their specific absence at the drain that evening any more than by the overall hatefulness of slavery or the distant promise of freedom in Florida brought closer by the looming prospect of war with Spain. The trigger for the escalating violence of that

---

16. Saidiya V. Hartman, *Scenes of Subjection: Terror, Slavery, and Self-Making in Nineteenth-Century America* (New York: Oxford, 1997), 22; Wood, *Slavery in Colonial America*, 63–64; Morgan, *Slave Counterpoint*, 387–388.

night was not an ideology of freedom and had nothing to do with an Atlantic world uprising of pirates, urban radicals, and proletarian bands against emerging capitalism's evils. The work crew's plan—to break into a store and obtain what they thought was their due for a hard day's labor—would evolve as the night wore on into something most of them had not planned. Efforts to escape the scene of accidental mayhem at the store would lead to more mayhem. The uproar, abetted by some slaves' efforts to gain aid from neighboring plantation slaves, would recruit a body of men who had not been part of the work crew, and these men's motives would differ from the diggers'.[17]

In all, then, most likely it was contingency that marked every step of the Stono Rebellion. Contingency is a synonym for chance. As a matter of fact, as Eugene Genovese has taught us, "Many revolts began as more or less spontaneous acts of despera-tion." But such desperation was common, whereas revolts are not. Contingency requires a trigger. Many little things coming together may tip the scales. In *The Tipping Point*, the popular sociologist and reporter Malcolm Gladwell explained how "change so often happens...quickly and...unexpectedly." Relating a series of case

17. My reconstruction of the events is based on the surviving evidence, comparative studies, an educated surmise, and Occam's razor, which holds that the simplest explanation of a complex but obscure sequence of events is probably the correct one. But see the argument in Peter Linebaugh and Marcus Rediker, *The Many-Headed Hydra: Sailors, Slaves, Commoners and the Hidden History of the Revolutionary Atlantic* (London: Verso, 2000), 198 and after, that Stono was part of a general proletarian uprising; and Justin Pope, "Dangerous Spirit of Liberty: The Spread of Slave Resistance in the British Atlantic, 1729–1742," paper read at the McNeil Center for Early American Studies, Philadelphia, January 15, 2010.

studies of epidemics and similar events, Gladwell suggested that "things can happen all at once, and little changes can make a huge difference." The tipping point—the big change—comes when enough little changes have occurred to tip the balance, and trigger a big change. "It's the boiling point. It's the moment on the graph when the line starts to shoot straight upwards."[18]

No one at the time knows when or how many of these little changes are necessary for the big change. But put them together and the unexpected at the time becomes the inevitable in hindsight. Think of the events at Stono as the moment when an outbreak of a contagious disease becomes a true epidemic. A few slaves were infected with simmering anger. They rehearsed their grievances large (at the outrage of slavery itself, at being away from home, at the impositions of white racism) and small (harbored against a particular overseer or master). The talk heated up as the heat of the day passed. A few voices were louder than the rest, and more insistent. Perhaps the speakers were natural leaders or had a physical presence that caused others to listen. The conversation took on a dramatic form, a kind of improvised script, with particular slaves playing roles they had rehearsed before this evening. There were leading actors and bit players.[19]

Now we can return to the crew as it approached Hutchenson's. Surely the trip had further whetted thirst and appetite unslaked

18. Eugene Genovese, *From Rebellion to Revolution: Afro-American Slave Revolts in the Making of the Modern World* (Baton Rouge: Louisiana State University Press, 1979), 3; Malcolm Gladwell, *The Tipping Point: How Little Things Can Make a Big Difference* (Boston: Little, Brown, 2000), introduction.

19. Wood, *Black Majority*, 200, 207, 213.

during the day's hard labor. The slave diggers might have brought some sustenance with them, and they had to drink or they would collapse from heat prostration, but now their thoughts likely turned to what they were owed in food and drink. Hutchenson's store was nearby, and they had visited it on occasion.[20]

What did they expect to do at Hutchenson's? Surely they would resume their conversation. Passing around a jug, belly full, men boasted of what they would do, could do, to those who had wronged them. In the New York City slave trials of 1741, slaves testified that after hours they gathered and boasted of feats of strength and cunning. They told stories and sang songs about far-off places they had known and exchanged tales of sexual prowess. It would not have been unthinkable for them to have offered grandiose plans for revenge and revolt. The target of the verbalized violence probably varied from night to night, depending on who was leading the conversation. For slaves who had little of their own, even the meanest planter home seemed a palace filled

---

20. How do we know that the slaves on the crew were hungry and thirsty? Slaves normally worked from sunup to sundown on these crews. They did not eat a dinner meal until they returned to their quarters. Individual slaves might leave off work when they could to find food or drink, but a day's work in late summer in the Low Country was thirsty and hungry work. One of the most evocative chroniclers of slavery, Charles Waddell Chestnutt, an African American author and lecturer, wrote in an 1899 short story, "in slab'ry times, a nigger did n' mine goin fi' or ten mile we'n dey wuz sump'n good ter eat at de yuther een." The speaker was fictional—Old Julius McAdoo, a former slave—but the recollection was true enough in its way, for Chestnutt's sources were former slaves, and he treated their recollections with empathy and dignity. Chestnutt, *The Conjure Woman* (Boston: Houghton Mifflin, 1899), 14.

with ornaments, food, and drink. Hutchenson's would substitute for the planters' homes, and with its supply of food and drink apportioned among themselves, the diggers could, at least for one night, imagine themselves their own masters.[21]

The first of the slave diggers arrived at Hutchenson's store, where they were surprised to find Robert Bathurst, most likely a servant or laborer, and John Gibbs, a prominent landowner, inside. Bathurst may have been hired as a night watchman. There is no record of his owning or renting land in Colleton. Oglethorpe called him "Mr." but that was an honorific title that he may not have deserved. Gibbs was a commissioner of highways (a job the legislature imposed on major planters). He had surveyed and claimed by memorial in 1732 a little more than fifteen hundred acres in Colleton and somewhat more in Berkeley County. He might have been in charge of the drainage job and left early to slake his own thirst from the store's supply of drink.[22]

The store was not open for business when the two men sat in it, and one can only surmise that they had private business to transact, or perhaps had shared one too many jugs themselves. One supposes they did not belong there, and that they would, in a very

21. Much of the passage here is surmise, but it is based on a wide variety of documentary evidence about slave uprisings in the eighteenth century. See, e.g., Hoffer, *Great New York Conspiracy*, 104–129; Herbert Aptheker, *American Negro Slave Revolts* (New York: International Publishers, 1943); Mullin, *Africa in America*; and Michael Craton, *Testing the Chains, Resistance to Slavery in the British West Indies* (Ithaca, N.Y.: Cornell University Press, 1982), 99–160.

22. John Gibbs, memorial, 1732, Series S111001, vol. 5, SCDAH; Highway Act of 1721, *Laws of the Province of South Carolina* (Charles Town, 1736), 361.

short time, bring terrible consequences. Had candlelight shown in the windows, the slaves might not have dared approach. But the only light was the dim and flickering remnant of a fire in the fireplace. Sweet-smelling whale-oil candles were expensive, and cheap tallow candles stank. Bathurst and Gibbs carried on their business by the dying embers of the fire. It is possible, but not likely, that the two men were not in the store when the break-in occurred but rushed there from somewhere nearby to investigate, and burst in on the slaves. But there is no evidence in the record that the store was one of a group of buildings. Where would the two whites have come from? There is another possibility of course. Gibbs was a supervisor on the roads commission charged with the drainage job. Bathurst may have been his assistant. It is possible, a purely speculative possibility, that they were in charge of the drainage job and left the work site early to repair to Hutchenson's.[23]

Whatever Bathurst and Gibbs were doing when the break-in occurred, the slaves could not risk being detected. Burglary (breaking into a dwelling at night with the intent to commit a crime) was a capital offense. Slaves were often accused of breaking into

---

23. An Account of the Negroe Insurrection in South Carolina," *Colonial Records of the State of Georgia*, ed. Allen D. Candler, William L. Northern, and Lucian L. Knight (Atlanta: Byrd, 1913) vol. 22 (part 2): 232–236; land grant memorials, 1732, South Carolina Department of Archives and History. What a terrible irony it would have been if Gibbs and Bathurst were supposed to be supervising the drainage crew. Then the confrontation would have had a much more personal tone. Both sides would have thought and perhaps even said, "What are you doing here?" The slaves who entered the store first would have known that they had no chance to escape blame for the break-in, because Gibbs would have known them. If this admittedly speculative scenario were true, then the slaves had no choice but to kill both the whites.

warehouses, storerooms, and even homes to steal food, drink, and clothing. Slave crime was a constant feature of slave colonies, and most slaves' crimes occurred on the plantation. One South Carolina planter burst into a dwelling in the quarters and found the entire shack filled with stolen goods, but most often the pilfered items were soon consumed or hidden. Crimes of violence against whites were rare, however, and violent assaults on other slaves often went unreported. On a few occasions, Low Country masters who wanted to save slaves from the death penalty for theft hid the slaves from the law, or moved them around from plantation to plantation.[24]

What happened in the store, we cannot know. Were the whites drowsy and killed before they could defend themselves? Did they put up a fight—the two groups knowing that the fight could only end in death? Were there words and threatening gestures that preceded the blows—and could the mortal result have been averted? We know only that the two whites were slain.

The murder of a white person in the Low Country by a slave was four times more common than in Virginia (the South Carolina assembly voted "half again as many" compensations to owners for the execution of their slaves, despite the fact that the slave population of Virginia was twice that of South Carolina for most of the century). Comparative figures computed by later historians could not have mattered much to the slaves or their victims. There is no mention in the record that the two whites slew any of their assailants, which may mean that the victims were asleep.[25]

24. Kulikoff, *Tobacco and Slaves*, 390–391; Morgan, *Slave Counterpoint*, 112–113, 266.

25. Morgan, *Slave Counterpoint*, 61, 395.

Under South Carolina law, the slaves were also guilty of "petty treason," the moment they delivered the mortal blows to the two whites. Taking part in a conspiracy to commit petty treason was also a capital crime. But even if the law regarded the murders as treason, which would have made the slaves into rebels, those slaves who struck the fatal blows did not yet want to mount a general uprising. Their thoughts turned to the problem of getting out of the mess alive. A slave traveling with a Georgia ranger reported a week and a half after the break-in that the killers "cut [the white men's] heads off and set them on the stairs." This was the only mention of decapitation in any of the accounts, and may be unreliable. In any case, cutting off heads did not require the actions of more than one man.[26]

26. "A Ranger's Report of Travels with General Oglethorpe, 1739–1742," *Travels in the American Colonies*, ed. Newton D. Mereness (New York: Macmillan, 1916), 222–223. Africans might decapitate to deny a soul the chance to return to the spirit world—a terrible fate (see Douglas Egerton, "A Particular Mark of Infamy: Dismemberment, Burial, and Rebelliousness in Slave Societies" in *Mortal Remains: Death in Early America*, ed. Nancy Isenberg and Andrew Burstein [Philadelphia: University of Pennsylvania Press, 2002], 154). The same slave, quoted in the ranger's report, said that the militia cut off the heads of the rebel leaders and displayed them. Again, this was the only mention of decapitation of the rebels, although in other cases, slave rebels were dismembered and displayed. In the Surinam slave rebellion of 1730, Dutch forces killed and displayed rebels: "The head shall then be severed and displayed on a stake by the riverbank…the Negro girls…will be tied to a cross, to be broken alive, and then their heads severed, to be exposed by the riverbank on stakes" (Richard Price, *Alabi's World* [Baltimore: Johns Hopkins University Press, 1990], 24). For the same reason—to make the masters' absolute dominion visible for miles around—the justices of the

The slaves took guns and ammunition from the store. They knew they would be pursued, and some among them had used guns to hunt. Even if some of the slaves wanted to steal guns rather than rum, even if they had planned, or harbored the plan, of escape, much less rebellion, who could have expected the store to be occupied so late at night? The victims, then, should not be counted as the first of many whites to die in a rebellion, but as two men in the wrong place at the wrong time.[27]

Whether the enslaved men were simply looking for a late-night frolick or planning some form of rebellion from the moment they set their feet on the path to the store, the murders were not anticipated as the first step in a grand design of rebellion. Thus, in a way, Gibbs's and Bathurst's deaths were the turning points, ironic causes of a rebellion they surely would have feared had they lived. Had they not been in the store after hours, they would not have died. Had the slaves not killed the two whites, their raid might have gone undetected. Perhaps they would have gotten away with the break-in, or perhaps they would have been caught after they returned to their plantations. Whichever of those events ensued, there would have

peace in colonial Alexandria, Virginia, used the courthouse chimney as the display case for the severed heads of four slaves executed for "petty treason" in 1767. A. Leon Higginbotham and Anne F. Jacobs, "'The Law Only as an Enemy': The Legitimation of Racial Powerlessness through the Colonial and Antebellum Criminal Laws of Virginia," *North Carolina Law Review* 70 (1992), 1039.

27. "An Account of the Negroe Insurrection in South Carolina," *Colonial Records of the State of Georgia*, ed. Allen D. Candler, William L. Northern, and Lucian L. Knight (Atlanta: Byrd, 1913), vol. 22 (part 2): 232–236.

been no general uprising. But the irony does not end here, not for Bathurst and Gibbs. "Wrong place, wrong time" was for them a death sentence, and the beginning of a night of terrors.[28]

Faced with the enormity of their unplanned actions, some of the slaves probably followed the lead of other members of the crew who had earlier vanished, reappearing in the quarters as though nothing had happened. If such slaves were not carrying weapons when they returned, they were likely to be excused or believed by their masters not to have had a part in the events. But those slaves who returned to the quarters after the murders spread the word of the murders among others in nearby houses, and no doubt revealed as well that some of the drain crew who had not left Hutchenson's had moved on in their thinking to a more general, and violent, form of resistance.[29]

28. Marvin Wolfgang, *Patterns in Criminal Homicide* (Philadelphia: University of Pennsylvania Press, 1958), 203–265, discusses the victim-induced homicide, in which the actions of the victim play a crucial role in the decision of the perpetrator. The victim puts himself in harm's way. The commonsense version of this is: do not leave the key to the car in the ignition.

29. For parallel situations in which plans were revealed or discussed, Anthony E. Kaye, *Joining Places: Slave Neighborhoods in the Old South* (Chapel Hill: University of North Carolina Press, 2007), 135–136; Winthrop D. Jordan, *Tumult and Silence at Second Creek: An Inquiry into a Civil War Slave Conspiracy*, rev. ed. (Baton Rouge: Louisiana State University Press, 1995), 212–213; James Sidbury, *Ploughshares into Swords: Race, Rebellion, and Identity in Gabriel's Virginia, 1730–1810* (Cambridge: Cambridge University Press, 1997), 100; Douglas R. Egerton, *He Shall Go out Free: The Lives of Denmark Vesey* (Madison, Wisc.: Madison House, 1999), 133; Marjolene Kars, "Rebellion, Civil War, and Revolution in Dutch Berbice, 1763–1764," paper read to the Conference on Atlantic Emancipations, Philadelphia, April 12, 2008, 14, quoted with permission of the author.

Some of the crew did not return to their plantations, fearing perhaps that their part in the planning or the execution of the break-in would be revealed by those who had run. Slaves routinely reported other slaves' infractions for the rewards or out of resentment or for motives only they knew. Those who stayed had now to decide: flee or fight? Of course, these were always options, and every day that slavery existed, according to the historian Winthrop Jordan, "freedom wore the red cap of bloody rebellion, and the colonists never doubted for a moment that their slaves might suddenly clap it to their heads."[30]

Colonial authorities, frightened periodically at the prospect of large-scale resistance, issued warnings about rebellion meant to spur the masters' watchfulness and to reinvigorate the patrols. But the historical fact is that individual slaves did not commit crimes of violence against their masters in anywhere near numbers comparable to the violent crimes that free persons committed against one another (or slaves committed against one another). Slaves seeking freedom (or revenge) did not don the red cap of rebellion. It was their masters in 1776 who joined the ranks of bloody rebellion in great numbers.[31]

In all likelihood the slaves remaining at Hutchenson's after the death of Bathurst and Gibbs debated what to do next. What they did not do is an important clue to their motives at

30. Jordan, *White over Black*, 111; Lathan A. Windley, *A Profile of Runaway Slaves in Virginia and South Carolina from 1730 through 1787* (New York: Garland, 1995), 107–129.

31. The relative absence of slave rebellions in early America is a fact. See, e.g., Peter C. Hoffer and Will B. Scott, *Criminal Proceedings in Colonial Virginia*, American Legal Records, Volume 10 (Athens: University of Georgia Press, 1984), xlvi–l, lviii; Morgan, *Slave Counterpoint*, 398.

the time. They did not set the store afire. Burning would have been an act of rebellion. Arson was seen by all and targeted the system of slavery itself. Burning destroyed what the master most valued: his habiliments and the chattel within them. Fire was so common in slave rebellions as to be symbolic of them. But no one set the store afire. Nor did they shoot off the firearms they now possessed. That, too, was common in a rebellion but at Hutchenson's would have called attention to the slaves. If a rebellion was planned, fire and gunshots would have signaled it. In short, if rebellion is an open call to resistance to a regime, the slaves who remained in the store did not yet portray themselves as rebels.[32]

So when did these slaves become rebels? The answer requires revisiting the chronology of the events. According to a report

32. On fires in slave rebellion, see Antoine Dalmas, on the 1791 rebellion in Saint-Domingue, quoted in *Slave Revolution in the Caribbean, 1789–1804: A Brief History with Documents*, by Laurent Dubois and John D. Garrigus (Boston: Bedford, 2006), 92. Setting fires and stealing firearms were part of the plan that Gabriel formulated to subdue Richmond and begin his rebellion in 1800. Sidbury, *Ploughshares into Swords*, 67. Kenneth Stampp, *The Peculiar Institution: Slavery in the Ante-bellum South* (New York: Knopf, 1956), 127–128, argues that arson was the slave's prime weapon against the oppressive master. Michael Meranze, *Laboratories of Virtue: Punishment, Revolution, and Authority in Philadelphia, 1760–1835* (Chapel Hill: University of North Carolina Press, 1996), 31, agrees. Slave arson was a felony and punishable by death throughout the colonies. Thomas D. Morris, *Southern Slavery and the Law* (Chapel Hill: University of North Carolina Press, 1996), 330–331. Masters in South Carolina particularly feared arson by slaves. Michael Stephen Hindus, *Prison and Plantation: Crimes, Justice, and Authority in Massachusetts and South Carolina, 1767–1878* (Chapel Hill: University of North Carolina Press, 1980), 144. Arson was a time-honored part of all slave rebellions. See, e.g., Mullin, *Africa in America*, 255. On the patrols, see Hadden, *Slave Patrols*, 22–23.

from the time, "Next they plundered and burnt Mr. Godfrey's house, and killed him, his daughter and son. They then turned back and marched southward along Pons Pon [*sic*] which is the road from Georgia to Augustine, they passed Mr. Wallace's tavern towards day break, and said they would not hurt him, for he was a good man and kind to his slaves." They did not go to John Williams's plantation nearby, though some of the slaves belonged to him. They did not descend upon William Bull's plantation on the Horse Savannah, though it abutted the drain and Bull was the richest man in the county. They did not, yet, act like rebels. Instead, "they turned back." Where and why "back"?[33]

To review the sequence again in more detail: First, the slaves went to Godfrey's, a house owned until a few years earlier by Benjamin Godfrey, a planter. When he died in 1734 his sons John and Richard inherited his properties. Both men lived in St. Pauls' Parish, Colleton, John on the North Edisto, Richard just across the Stono from Johns Island. Richard's land was close to the Main Road and Hutchenson's store and Wallace's tavern. John's place on the North Edisto had a "landing," the terminus of a road running from the north branch of the Stono through St. Johns' and St. Pauls' parishes, but given its location, surely Richard's plot had a landing on the Stono as well.[34]

<hr />

33. "An Account of the Negroe Insurrection in South Carolina," 233; William Bull memorial, 1733, series S111001, vol. 2, SCDAH.

34. Caroline T. Moore and Agatha Aimar Simmons, eds., *Abstracts of the Wills of the State of South Carolina, 1670–1740* (Charlotte, N.C. n.p., 1960), 138; "An Act for Making a New Road between the North and the Middle Branch of the Stono River," 1734, *Laws of the Province of South Carolina*, 464; Richard Godfrey's land appeared at the edge of the plat for Stephen Monk granted to John Monk for 320 acres in Colleton, near the Stono River. See plat books, S213184, SCDAH.

Slaves seeking to depart quietly and in haste from Hutchenson's naturally made for Godfrey's landing hoping to find some means of waterborne transportation away from the scene. Some among the fugitives must have been boatmen or fishermen. They knew that the Stono and the North Edisto ran to the sea and that somewhere across that great body of water lay home. But whatever means of waterborne escape they imagined, whether simply a dash from the scene of the crime, a voyage down the coast to Spanish Florida, or even a chance to sail home, something went wrong. Perhaps there were no boats or not enough to accommodate them. Perhaps one of the Godfrey family discovered them. Or one of them may have harbored some grievance against the Godfreys to begin with, and arrived with malice in mind. Perhaps only a combination of actions and reactions unplanned and unfortunate led to the death of Godfrey's family. Whatever happened at Godfrey's place, the die was now truly cast against the slaves' undetected escape, and the slaves on the scene burned the house.

Although none of the contemporary accounts mentions this fact, slaves must have taken lanterns from Hutchenson's. The lantern (or "lanthorne") was a craft item long in use in England. The cheaper lanterns, tin frames with candleholders, and the more expensive variety, candle or oil lanterns of iron or copper with glass windows, would have been much prized items at Hutchenson's. Unlike the torch, which throws its light out and up, the lantern can be held below the waist, and there lights the ground below and ahead. The lantern, dangerous for runaways, was a perfect aid to the rebels on foot.[35]

---

35. Hayward, *Colonial Lighting*, 55–74. For me, a flashlight is a welcome aid when hiking at night, even when I am following a well-beaten path in a field.

Site of Wallace Tavern (photograph by author).

Wallace's tavern lay not far from Godfrey's and Hutchenson's, most likely at a landing where the Wallace Creek (now the Wallace River) crossed Pon Pon Road (now US 17). The site was occupied in 2008 by the Paradise Bar and Grill (formerly the Club Ron Da Vue). In all probability Wallace's was little more than a tippling house. Slaves were not by law to visit these or to buy liquor, but they did. Sellers of liquor were to be licensed, but some escaped this regulation. There is nothing of Wallace's tavern in the surviving records, but if it lay near Pon Pon Road, it would have been a welcome stop for travelers. Wallace himself may have been the William Wallace who reappeared in 1740 as a Charles Town importer of "general merchandise," wisely not chancing his luck in the countryside.[36]

Wallace had friends among the slaves who visited that night and probably knew about the fracas at the store before any other white man. If he sold liquor, he knew that he might be robbed, and kept arms nearby. Likely again, he owned or leased a slave or two, but the hint in the records that he was spared because he had been "good" to his slaves does not make complete sense, unless the slaves who came to his door were not the same slaves who "plundered" Godfrey's house. And what was he doing in his tavern that early in the morning? If he lived there, he was awakened. Possibly his slaves had warned him, and he was ready for the visit. These last conjectures enable us to make a little more sense of the events that night. Slaves from the store had spread out over the county, and each breakaway cadre from the main body had its own purposes.[37]

It was now "daybreak." The primary sources listing the victims put the house attacks into chronological order, suggesting that a single group of slaves was attacking houses one after another along Pon Pon Road. But the two-dimensional chronology on the printed page has a spurious linearity and completeness. The order of the attacks may not have been correct, for they were far more likely not in sequence but roughly simultaneous. This alternative reading of the events would explain how a body of slaves could fly over the land with great speed, alighting at various dark-

---

36. Stuart O. Stumpf, "South Carolina Importers of General Merchandise, 1735–1765," *South Carolina Historical Magazine* 84 (1983), 6.

37. Hoffer, *Great New York Conspiracy*, 62, 72, 85.

ened houses set in distant spots, accomplishing so much in so little time. It makes sense that the remainder of the drain crew, becoming both bolder and more desperate, broke into smaller bands and went in different directions.

Some of those paths led to sheer tragedy. "They broke open and plundered Mr. Lemy's house, and killed him, his wife and child." Lemy was likely a renter; there is no record of his seeking to patent land. He may have owned a few slaves; most white land-holders did, for even if they grew little rice, they needed field labor to survive at all (given the mortality rate of their own children). Saturday was a workday for Lemy and his family. He would have toiled in the fields while his wife labored closer to home. She had risen early to stir the embers and restart the fire, empty the chamberpots, draw the water, and prepare and then serve the first meal. The rest of her day was more of the same: clothing to mend, children to watch, household duties to perform, livestock to feed and tend, and nursing if there was an infant. Bone tired by the evening, husband and wife would be looking forward to the Sabbath and meeting neighbors at church, though Sunday morning church meant clean clothes and another early morning's work.[38]

They retired early on Saturday night, because for them, as for Bathurst and Gibbs, lighting candles was too expensive. With the light gone, sounds became more important. The early modern

38. "An Account of the Negroe Insurrection," 228; on slaveholding by yeoman farmers, see Stephanie McCurry, *Masters of Small Worlds: Yeoman Households, Gender Relations, and the Political Culture of the Antebellum South Carolina Low Country* (New York: Oxford University Press, 1995), 48; Adam Rothman, *Slave Country: American Expansion and the Origins of the Deep South* (Cambridge, Mass.: Harvard University Press, 2005), 186–187.

night was full of noise and the summer night in rural South Carolina had its share of animal and insect howls, shrieks, rustles, whirrs, and thumps. Wooden cabins creak and groan. Half asleep, the couple noted the familiar sounds. Poorer homesteaders' houses had either two rooms, one for sleeping and the other for food production and storage, or four, adding a good room or parlor for receiving visitors and a second bedroom. Lemy and his family probably slept on the ground floor. What did the couple hear before their killers burst into their room? Did a family dog bark? Did a servant yell a warning? Did they have time to put up a defense, find a weapon, strike a blow? Or were the Lemys overcome and dispatched in a few terrible moments of terror and pain?

Then the rebels "marched on toward Mr. Rose's, resolving to kill him but he was saved by a Negro, who having hid him went out and pacified the others." This slave was Wells, a trusted and loved member of the Rose household. When another group of slaves marched on Thomas Elliott's home, July and other bondmen there armed themselves and warned off the marauders.[39]

Perhaps July and those who joined in him staving off the marauders might be seen as traitors to their class, race, and fellow sufferers. Certainly the celebration of July's actions and the rewards given other loyal slaves after the uprising by the master class support this judgment. At the same time, would it not be an

---

39. Thomas Rose, will, May 25, 1756, wills book, 1752–1756, p. 518, SCDAH; Morgan, *Slave Counterpoint*, 268; November 29, 1739, *Journal of the Commons House of Assembly, September 12, 1739–March 26, 1741*, pp. 62–63.

act of genuine courage and loyalty to a family with whom one lived to save them from the murderous rage of a violent crew? Every slave in St. John and St. Paul had to make this choice before the day was over, some more than once. It was not an easy choice for any of them.[40]

But the most telling motive of slaves making their choice was a rational calculation of the likely success of the uprising. Slaves born in the colony or well versed in the white power structure's ability to protect itself might decide that the rebels had no future and that anyone who came to their aid would be summarily executed. That is what happened to anyone suspected of joining in the rebellion after it was over—so that calculation proved to be a correct one. Some slaves who hated slavery and despaired of their own condition might still have been motivated by personal attachment to a family member. Why let some slave one did not know break into a house and harm people one knew? Slaves who had some kinship relation to their owners (and the number of people of mixed ancestry in the colony was testimony of such kinship) would also protect half-brothers and -sisters from home invaders.

Throughout the night, fragments of the original band roamed over the southeastern end of the county. Rose lived near the North Branch of the Stono, near the bridge. Thomas Elliott Jr.'s lands lay on both sides of the Stono River, but Elliott lived south of the Stono, for he represented St. Johns in the assembly, not St. Pauls. Clearly, some of the rebels remained on the eastern side

40. November 29, 1739, *Journal of the Commons House of Assembly, September 12, 1739–March 26, 1741*, p. 62.

of Johns Island while others continued toward the west and the North Edisto River.[41]

The rebels destroyed the dwellings and killed both the inhabitants of yeoman farmsteads and rich planters. This was not class warfare. Slaves, at the bottom rung of the economic ladder, struck at the people one rung above, the poor farmer. Criminology offers an insight into the way in which the crime gives power to the powerless, but the victims are also powerless. Crimes such as housebreaking and even murder become symptomatic of the effects of oppression on both the criminal and the victim. For the poor renter lived little better than the slave in many material respects. Diet and housing were roughly equivalent. Certainly, life was equally perilous and labor equally burdensome. Above all, the poor renter did not have a cadre of slaves to protect him and his family.[42]

Accounts of Stono published many years after the event included lurid tales of the rebels' plan to ravish white women, but at the time and immediately after no accusation of this type was made. Rape was and is a form of subordination that conquerors deploy to demonstrate their absolute mastery over a conquered people. In other slave rebellions, rape did occur as the rebels

41. "An Act for Making a New Road," *Laws of the Province*, 464; Plot diagram for Jeremiah Miles's memorial, Series S213184, Plot for Thomas Miles, Series S213184, SCDAH.

42. On the victims and the victimizers, see Mark M. Linear and Stuart Henry, *Essential Criminality*, 2nd ed. (Boulder, Colo.: Westview, 2004), 279. On diet, compare Morgan, *Slave Counterpoint*, 92–93, and Mechal Sobel, *The World They Made Together: Black and White Values in Eighteenth-Century Virginia* (Princeton: Princeton University Press, 1987), 141–142; with McCurry, *Masters of Small Worlds*, 62–63.

either gained revenge for the rape of slave women or imagined themselves at the top of the social ladder. But not at Stono.[43]

Portions of the rebel band tried to recruit in the quarters. Slaves often traveled the countryside at night or in very early morning to visit other plantations, avoiding the patrols, and thus could have moved in this fashion on the night of September 8 and early the next morning. The scattered pattern of movement makes sense not only in terms of the victimization of the whites but in the attempt to attract other blacks to the project. If the rebels had been in the colony for a while, they knew which plantations were likely places to recruit and which were best avoided. The rebels must have had some success recruiting to have continued their efforts (and raised their hopes of a general uprising). By early morning the remaining members of the drain crew had not only replaced the crew members who had departed but had increased the number of rebels by thirty to forty slaves. The first report of the marchers on the road put their number at sixty.[44]

The distances the slaves traveled in the night and early morning in the course of attempting to recruit new troops may seem staggering. It is more than fifteen miles along the old course of Pon Pon Road from where Wallace Creek flows into the Stono to

43. The alleged conspiracy of the slaves at Second Creek in Mississippi, in 1861, included plans to rape white women. See Jordan, *Tumult and Silence*, 73. With a few exceptions, black men did not rape white women, and rape was not associated with slave revolts. Aptheker, *American Negro Slave Revolts*, 224. White men raping black women was not uncommon, however. See Jordan, *White over Black*, 153, 154.

44. I am grateful to Douglas Egerton for suggesting that the rebels' knowledge of the neighborhood directed their steps that night.

the crossing over the South Branch of the Edisto, or as described by the surveyors, the east side of the Pon Pon River. All night and early morning the rebels had to navigate through fields and across sodden wetlands. They crossed creeks. Even if they followed the contours of the Pon Pon after their assaults on the various plantations, they would have traveled more than fifteen miles that night. How was this possible?[45]

The Angolans, who constituted the majority of the slaves imported to South Carolina in the 1730s, counted among their number veteran foot soldiers. If the core of the pre-dawn raider band was Angolan and had fought in Africa, it would explain how they covered so much ground so quickly. European armies marched to battle in columns. Colonial militias rode on horseback. West African armies included a few cavalry units, but in the main African armies on the savannah, including West Central African range lands, ran to war.[46]

With the sun rising and the fiery effects of the evening's attacks becoming visible, "several Negroes joined [the band], they calling out liberty." The newcomers to the band were the slaves recruited during the night, and they in turn openly continued the recruiting activity: "[They] marched on with colors displayed, and two drums beating, pursuing all the white people they met with, and killing man woman and child when they could come up to them…. [They] burnt Colonel Hext's house and killed his

45. Slaves crossed rivers all the time to work fields on both sides of the water. Though they were not supposed to own canoes, they were boatmen and so valued that they were often allowed to ply the fishing and carting trade without white supervision. Morgan, *Slave Counterpoint*, 56, 241.

46. John K. Thornton, "African Dimensions of the Stono Rebellion," *American Historical Review* 96 (1991), 1101–1113.

overseer and his wife. They then burnt Mr. Sprye's house, then Mr. Sacheverell's. And Mr. Nash's house, all lying on the Pons Pon [*sic*] Road, and killed all the white people they found in them. Mr. Bullock got off, but they burnt his house."

Alexander Hext was the leading planter in the region. He served St. Johns Colleton in the assembly, and between 1731 and 1738 recorded more than 2,500 acres of purchases in Colleton, and nearly as much elsewhere. David and Edward Hext were also busy in the real estate business. Thomas Sacheverell was an important planter, as was Royal Sprye. Both men were involved in the land-speculation business, leasing and buying and selling. James Bullock was a justice of the peace, as was Alexander Hext, and was recorded as living at least part of the time in Willtown, on the east side of the South Edisto.[47]

47. "An Account of the Negroe Insurrection," 235. Alexander, David, and Edward were the sons of Hugh Hext. Alexander and David served in the assemblies during the 1730s. Commons Journal, *Journal of the Commons House of Assembly, November 10, 1736–June 7, 1739*, pp. 3, 5. Alexander's first recorded memorial for Colleton land was in 1731, for 500 acres. See Memorial Series 213184, p. 192, item 2, SCDAH. The purchases occurred once or twice every two years thereafter, and grew larger and larger, e.g., memorial for 1,000 acres, 1735, Series 213019, p. 489, SCDAH. Thomas Sacheverell will, January 22, 1745, wills 1740–1747, pp. 475–476, SCDAH; Moore and Simmons, eds., *Abstract of the Wills*, 178; Register of Mesne conveyance, deed books, copies in SCDAH, F283 (Sacheverell), S 247 (Sprye); F 326 (Bullock); *South Carolina Historical and Genealogical Magazine* 11 (1908), 189; A. S. Salley Jr., "Hugh Hext and Some of His Descendants," *South Carolina Historical and Genealogical Magazine* 6 (1905), 28–40. Note that the memorials were recorded in 1731–1733, before St. Johns Parish was created out of a portion of St. Pauls. Thus, many of the planters who lived on Edisto, Johns Island, or Wadmalaw Island were recorded in their memorials as living in St. Pauls.

But again, not every slave in the quarters—not even close to the majority of them—rallied to the rebel cause. Thomas Rose's slave Wells; the Wilkinson family's slaves; Thomas Elliott's slaves Ralph, Prince, Joe, Larush, and Pompey; and the slaves of Joseph Elliott, William Peters, the widow Wilkinson, John Tucker, and William Dandridge "behaved well" during the uprising, ignoring or resisting the rebels. Frederick Grimke's Pompey, Tony, and Primus had disdained the appeals of his other bondmen and protected their owner and his family. Henry Williamson's James and Benjamin Williamson's Scipio likewise choose not to rebel, and helped save their masters. John Smith's slaves were similarly divided, some choosing to revolt, others not only remaining loyal but physically contesting their former comrades. In the end, it was slave against slave in the early morning, not just slave against master.[48]

Pause for another moment. Were there drums? If the little army had drums, one might assume that perhaps the uprising was planned earlier. But homemade instruments could be found in most plantations' quarters. Slave woodworkers had no trouble fashioning the instruments. Singing and dancing to gourds, drums, and stringed instruments (forerunners of the banjo) were common entertainments that planters watched and applauded. The appearance of drums and drummers in the morning does not prove a prior conspiracy to raise the countryside. If the remnant of the drain crew recruited through the night, some of the recruits might indeed have brought instruments with them. The beating of drums then might well have called a message to other

48. Committee report, November 10, 1739, *Journal of the Commons House of Assembly, September 12, 1739–March 26, 1741,* pp. 63–64.

slaves, at least attracting their attention, but none of the accounts of the night suggest that slaves beat drums until the morning's parade down the Pon Pon.[49]

Rejoin the rebel band, now making little effort to conceal its progress. The rebel force was growing as it marched down Pon Pon road. But the men were tired from a night's racing from slave quarters to slave quarters over a wide area of Colleton, cajoling, threatening, boasting. They were in territory they did not know as well as they did the Wallace Creek area. Their victims were not the planters who sent slaves to dig the drain. Sacheverell did not live in St. Johns' Parish. He lived on the "west side of the Pon Pon River," hence in St. Pauls. Sprye lived on an estate called Saxbys, next to the North Branch of the Edisto.[50]

On the road, fatigue closed the rebel ranks. Infantry on the march, particularly after a long haul, will tend to bunch up. They have to be told to keep their spacing. The sunrise had made it easier for the body of men to come together, and for a newly "confident" leadership to emerge, but it also made plain to the slaves that they had not achieved their objective. There was no general uprising. They had killed two dozen whites, burned a dozen houses, and thrown the countryside into panic. Still, decisions

---

49. Morgan, *Slave Counterpoint*, 236, 419–420, 583.

50. Royal Sprye, will, December 17, 1746, wills book, 1740–1746, p. 614, SCDAH. Thomas Sacheverell, plat for land in Colleton County, S213184, plat book, SCDAH; Petition of Thomas Sacheverell and others, January 31, 1740, *Journal of the Commons House of Assembly, September 12, 1739–March 26, 1741*, ed. J. H. Easterby (Columbia, S.C., 1952), 165. The plat for land granted to Sacheverell shows on its border "Thomas Elliott's land." Elliott had pieces of land all over Colleton, however. He lived in St. Johns, not St. Pauls, because he was a representative to the assembly from St. Johns.

had to be made: Go on as a body and try to raise the countryside? Break again into smaller and swifter groups and avoid all contact with whites? Give it up and try to talk their way out of trouble back on their plantations? In the end, the number of committed individuals was sufficient for a hundred or so slaves to march on together down the Pon Pon toward Florida.[51]

❧

A series of accidental confrontations, framed by the violence inherent in slavery itself, had cascaded into a rebellion. As one misfortune for the slaves and their victims piled upon another, the leaders of the band had fewer and fewer choices. There was no safety for them, unless they won with a "single stroke." They lacked what is today called "operational intelligence," the knowledge in advance of the enemy's strength, deployment, and likely response. Overly optimistic because of their early successes, expecting perhaps that recruits would arrive in substantial numbers, and as yet unopposed by organized forces, the slaves marched down the road confidently.[52]

The above reconstruction of events—the most plausible at least to this author's mind—concludes that a drainage crew's desire for a party after days of working in the puff mud of Horse Savannah had led to a botched break-in at a store and two dead whites. Part of the crew left the scene and returned to their plantations. Another group sought to escape sure conviction and death for the murders, but there were no boats to carry them to safety at Godfrey's landing, and the house invasion led to more deaths. In

51. "An Account of the Negroe Insurrection in South Carolina," 234.
52. Genovese, *From Rebellion to Revolution*, 18.

the wake of these events, a plan was born to raise the countryside, and slaves traveled all over Johns, Wadmalaw, and Edisto islands seeking recruits. It was not a new plan, for surely slaves had contemplated such acts and even discussed them with other slaves before. As the recruiters and their new comrades gathered on Pon Pon Road, they left behind a burning countryside and more white victims. The plan now was to march to Florida and freedom, but a fight to the death was about to begin.[53]

53. But one cannot entirely dispose of the possibility of multiple partial explanations for the events at Hutchenson's and those that followed. Every slave might have had his own motivation. Fear, anger, pride, and hope all burned in the breasts of the enslaved that night and early morning. But it is also possible that the lure of freedom in Florida acted as a suppressant to slave revolt, for running away to Florida was a kind of safety valve for the slave system, drawing off those able and angry slaves who might otherwise become ringleaders of rebellions.

· *Four* ·

ON PON PON ROAD

❧

Pon Pon Road was a portion of the King's Highway linking Charles Town with Savannah. Of packed earth, thirty feet wide (twenty at the causeways), rutted and dusty, it ran from the Ashley, past the crossing over the Stono at Hutchenson's, to the South Branch of the Edisto and its crossing at Jacksonborough, and on west and south. Commissioners appointed in each parish to push the road through found that the overseers chosen to manage the work would rather forgo the fees and pay the fines than stand in the heat and humidity and watch the slave laborers, but the road was completed by 1739.[1]

Manly Williamson, whose plantation would most benefit from a clear-cut road and bridge across the Ashley, was named commissioner to see that the road and the bridges crossing it were unimpeded. He could also run, and charge fees, for a ferry. There is no record of his failing to ensure "quick and safe traveling of man and horse." He had kept the Pon Pon free of his neighbors' negli-

1. See, e.g., Complaint of William Webb and William Jackson, January 21, 1738, *Journal of the Commons House of Assembly, November 10, 1736–June 7, 1739*, ed. J. H. Easterby (Columbia, S.C., 1951), 401.

Pon Pon Road, today Jacksonborough Road (photograph by author).

gence, for planters often "stop up or obstruct" the roads with logs or ditches, and some villains "opposed the same commissioners" trying to mend and repair the roads. The commissioner's was a thankless task, best avoided, for the commissioner had to put up a bond for doing his job properly that would be forfeited if the roads and bridges were not clear, and he could only bring an action against the malefactors in the courts and there seek damages.[2]

Early on the morning of September 9, a column of armed men marched west along Pon Pon Road. In the troop, slaves from

2. "An Act for Cutting and Making a Path," *Journal of the Commons House of Assembly, November 10, 1736–June 7, 1739*, pp. 255–256.

Ann Drayton's, William Cattell's, and John Williams's plantations bordering the Horse Savannah walked alongside those from the plantations of Henry Williamson, Frederick Grimke, John Smith, Thomas Sacheverell, and Benjamin Wilkinson along the Stono. They were less than a disciplined troop and more than a ragged band of enslaved men, some exhausted but exhilarated from their night's labors, two drummers announcing their progression and a flag bearer at their head. They called out to others like them to join their enterprise, and some—but not many—had come. Surely by now, if not before, the band had a leader, or more likely, a group of leaders. Jemmy, or Cato, later accounts recalled, were the boldest and the most well spoken of the rebels.[3]

Later the planters would describe to the assembly what had happened: "The petitioners who were owners of slaves there had always taken the best care they possibly could for keeping them in good order and demeanor, as well by their own personal inspection as by employing overseers over them," a hint that in protesting too much about "best care" these planters were not the kindliest

3. For Cato, see David Ramsay, *History of South Carolina from Its First Settlement in 1670 to the Year 1808* (Newberry, S.C.: W. J. Duffie, 1858), 62; for Jemmy, see "An Account of the Negroe Insurrection in South Carolina," *Colonial Records of the State of Georgia*, ed. Allen D. Candler, William L. Northern, and Lucian L. Knight (Atlanta: Byrd, 1913) 22 (part 2): 233. The first rebels would have been drawn from plantations around the Horse Savannah. These included Ann Drayton's slaves, memorial, 1733, Series S111001, vol. 1, p. 485, South Carolina Department of Archives and History [SCDAH], Columbia, S.C.; John Williams's slaves, memorial, 1733, Series S213019, vol. 1, p. 134, William Cattell's slaves, memorial, 1733, Series S111001, vol. 3, p. 157. Others came later, for example from Thomas Sacheverell's plantation, memorial, 1735, Series S111001, vol. 5, p. 290, SCDAH.

of masters. The petitioners added that "as Negroes by nature are generally prone to cruelty, barbarity and savage endeavors, and that the like misfortune might as well have taken rise in any other part of the province where slaves were settled, and must be necessarily employed for raising provisions and commodities to support the inhabitants and trade of the country" the colony ought to repay the planters for the lost value of the rebels.[4]

In midmorning the lieutenant governor of the colony, William Bull, came upon the band. He was riding with four companions toward Charles Town from a session of the Granville district court. It was a long day's ride to Charles Town from Beaufort, not far from the Savannah River in the southwestern coastal corner of the colony, and the five men must have been tired. This may explain why they reacted as they did to the sight of a marching column of blacks coming toward them from Charles Town. For a moment, they did nothing, assuming perhaps that the band was a work crew. The drumming might be harmless, for slaves sometimes gathered on the Sabbath to dance and sing. Then the fires on the horizon and something about the manner of the band told a different story, and Bull's party galloped away.

Bull's is the only eyewitness account of any part of the events that survives. A sharp business acumen and his clever decision to court royal favor even before the colony became a Crown possession in 1729 had won him the post. His father, Stephen, a Welsh immigrant, made money in land speculation and married into more. Bull then "parlayed his small inheritance into a fortune" in rice, supplemented

4. Petition of Henry Williamson et al., January 31, 1741, *Journal of the Commons House of Assembly, September 12, 1739–March 26, 1741*, pp. 165–166.

by a land-surveying business (a good way to discover properties one might wish to purchase). He was not a seasoned administrator, though he had served in the legislature for years, and his term would end shortly after the events he witnessed.[5]

By the time he wrote his report of the meeting, Bull knew a great deal about the uprising, but in his account he confined himself to the bare bones: "On the 9th of September last at night a great number of Negroes arose in rebellion, broke open a store where they got arms, killed twenty-one white persons, and were marching the next morning in a daring manner out of the province, killing all they met, and burning several houses they passed along the road." He turned next to his own part in the events: "I was returning from Granville court [a session of a short-lived experiment with county law courts] with four gentlemen and met these rebels at eleven o'clock in the forenoon, and fortunately discerned the approaching danger time enough to avoid it."[6]

5. Geraldine M. Meroney, *Inseparable Loyalty: A Biography of William Bull* (Norcross, Ga.: Harrison, 1991), 12, 19; Plat of 400 acres laid out for Silas Wells...St. Paul's Parish, 1740, plat books, South Carolina Historical Society, Charleston, S.C.

6. William Bull to the Board of Trade, October 5, 1739, C.O. [Colonial Office] papers 1730–146, 5/388, copy in South Carolina Department of Archives and History, Columbia, S.C., Records in the British Public Record Office Pertaining to South Carolina, 1711–1782, vol. 20:179–180. Why had Bull waited so long to file his report? He had his own conduct to explain. Indeed, he must have worried about how to couch his role in the events, because when trouble came his way, he fled. What was more, Bull had telescoped the events of the evening and early morning, giving them a false unity and completeness. He had surely consulted white survivors and the militia, and perhaps even interviewed slaves, but he simply assumed that the band he saw was exactly the same as the crew that broke into Hutchenson's.

If they had left the Beaufort District, where the Granville court sat, after breakfasting (a likely course of action), Bull and his companions would have been tired by midmorning—apparently tired enough to blunder onto the head of the band without quite realizing what was happening. The slaves on foot and Bull and his cohort on horseback, the lieutenant governor and his little troop were able to flee safely. Even as they spurred away, Bull and his companions must have wondered how many slaves would join the little army. The terror of a general uprising gave purpose to their flight as they took off in different directions to alert the countryside to the danger threatening it.

Bull's report is tersely written. It was penned many weeks after the events, surely enough time for him to gather evidence, interview victims, and perhaps even interrogate suspected rebels. He included nothing of this in the report, in all likelihood because his own actions that day did not put him in a good light. Instead of confronting the band and ordering them to disperse, or himself leading the militia against them, he fled. There is no evidence that he took part in the military actions that day or later, though his appointment as acting lieutenant governor included a commission as the commanding officer of the militia.

A little after noon, having progressed about fifteen miles west along the Pon Pon from Wallace Creek, the rebel band stopped to rest and celebrate their achievement. Common sense tells us that they must have been almost completely exhausted, both emotionally and physically. Traveling such a distance in the morning, added to their evening's activity, was taking its toll. Their state of mind and body would have an important influence on the rest of the day's events.[7]

According to Oglethorpe, after it appeared that the rebels had driven off Bull, "they increased every minute by new Negroes coming to them, so that they were above sixty, some say a hundred, on which they halted in a field, and set to dancing. Singing and beating drums, to draw more Negroes to them, thinking that they were now victorious over the whole province [of South Carolina] having marched ten miles and burnt all before them without opposition." Tired, they nonetheless celebrated. Why not? Until the wee hours of the morning they were slaves. Now they were once again free men. If Bull saw them, surely they saw him flee. Would this not have increased their confidence? In addition, every slave coming into the field were the rebels stopped buoyed their hopes of eventual success. The rebel leaders might have made a critical error here, mistaking curiosity seekers and onlookers for recruits. Two years later, in the course of a report on the war with Spanish Florida, the South Carolina assembly concluded that the rebels had become overconfident at the lack of resistance. The report overlooked the likelihood that many, if not most, of the slaves in the field had arrived long after the killing and burning, and had come to watch the proceedings, and perhaps join in the revelry.[8]

7. Roddie Burris, "Failed Uprising Resulted in Harsher Life for Slaves," *Columbia State*, February 2, 2003, B6. The distances are my own calculation.

8. "An Account of the Negroe Insurrection in South Carolina," 234–235; "Report of the Committee Appointed to Enquire into the Causes of the Disappointment of Success in the Late Expedition against St. Augustine," July 1, 1741, *Journal of the Commons House of Assembly, May 18, 1741-July 10, 1742*, ed. J. H. Easterby (Columbia, S.C., 1953), 84.

What if the main body of the rebels had not stopped in the field, but had sped down the Pon Pon toward the Savannah River. Could they have inspired others to join them in flight? Would the march become a mass "exodus," Jemmy and Cato leading their people from slavery to freedom? The answer, again, relies upon simple common sense. Given that most of the slaves, and probably the leadership, were exhausted, such dispatch would have drained their last reserves of energy. What is more, if the main body marched on and increasing numbers of the band fell behind, the stragglers would have been easy prey for the militia, coming down the road. In any case, slaves on foot could not out-run the mounted militia. Had the slaves pressed on, they could not have escaped their fate. And that fate was already on its way.[9]

9. Ramsay, *History of South Carolina*, 62. Ira Berlin's account of Stono in his much-acclaimed *Many Thousands Gone*: The First Two Centuries of Slavery in North America (Cambridge, Mass.: Harvard University Press, 1998), calls the march an exodus: "In 1739 a group of African slaves initiated a mass exodus. Pursued by South Carolina militiamen, the fugitives confronted their owners' soldiers in several pitched battles at Stono, only fifty miles from the Florida border" (p. 73). The account errs in numerous ways. The march was not an exodus. In an exodus, an entire people, or at least a segment of an entire people, pick up and leave. At Stono there were no women or children among the rebels, and there is no hint in the primary sources that women and children joined the march. Had the battle at Stono been but fifty miles from the Florida border, perhaps many more slaves would have taken a chance on joining the rebels. But the battle was nowhere near Florida. The Stono itself is never more than twenty-five miles from Charleston. The Savannah River, the Georgia border, is about eighty miles by sea (or as the crow flies) from Charleston. From the Georgia border to St. Augustine is a little more than 150 miles, again on the most direct route. But for the slaves, avoiding white settlements such as Beaufort and Savannah would have required detours into the interior and many extra miles.

Bull reported that he "gave notice to the militia."[10] He was taking credit, again, that he did not deserve. In fact, it was one of Bull's four gentlemen, an aptly named Mr. Golightly (possibly Fenwick Golightly), who flew to the Presbyterian Church at Willtown to sound the alarm. The Pon Pon ran at a right angle to the road to Willtown. Willtown itself was laid out as a defensive post, little more than a fort and haven for whites in the Yamasee Indian wars of 1713–1716. By the 1720s it had become a village, and a decade later, as rice culture made the Low Country a major rice producer, Willtown became a "flourishing" town. Today, the "footprints" of the colonial town's buildings are still visible, about eight miles down the south fork of the Edisto from the King's Highway.[11]

Golightly brought the news of the rebellion to the worshipers at the Willtown Presbyterian church. The colony was officially within the jurisdiction of the Church of England—that is, it had an "established church" to which everyone paid dues. Anglican missionaries from the Society for the Propagation of the Gospel in Foreign Parts held services for planters, slaves, and Indians. But the congregants at Willtown had their own "dissenting" church. If it resembled the Johns Island Presbyterian Church first erected in 1719, it was a plain clapboard boxlike structure of two stories, the simple interior's wooden pews facing a low pulpit. None of the soaring steeples or high altars of the Church of England for

10. William Bull to the Board of Trade, October 5, 1739.
11. "An Act for Cutting and Making a Path...to the Town of Wilton in Colleton County," 1711, *Earliest Laws*, 253–254; Martha Zierden, Suzanne Linder, and Ronald Anthony, *Willtown: An Archeological and Historical Perspective* (Charleston, S.C.: Charleston Museum, 1999), 2–7.

Johns Island Presbyterian Church (photograph by author).

these dissenters. Independent-minded and pious in their own fashion, they might not have been the most prosperous planters, but they belonged to the planter class.[12]

Out of the church poured the militiamen, led by Captain John Bee. He was a planter of substance and a man of sincere religious convictions. A migrant from Northern Ireland of Scottish descent,

12. Ramsay, *History of South Carolina*, 62; Peter Wood, *Black Majority: Negroes in Colonial South Carolina through the Stono Rebellion* (New York: Norton, 1973), 133–142; William P. Baldwin Jr. et al., *Plantations of the Low Country: South Carolina, 1697–1865* rev. ed. (Greensboro, N.C.: Legacy, 1987), 29–30.

Bee had come to Colleton early in the century and accumulated more than a thousand acres in a series of small grants. He lived next to Sprye and Sacheverell, who counted him a good neighbor and friend. Bee married the youngest daughter of Hugh Hext, connecting him and his family to one of the most important clans in the region. Bee was a founding member of the Willtown Presbyterian church in 1731. When elected to the legislature from St. Pauls' Parish, Colleton County, in 1742, he refused to take the oath required of all officeholders that the Anglican Church was the one true church. He would swear only that he was a good Christian.[13]

The law required white male churchgoers to carry arms to their churches. Sometimes, they left the arms at the door in the care of trusted slaves. Others did not part with the weapons. The irony of leaving firearms with house servants who accompanied the worshipers was obvious, as was the preaching of the gospel of Jesus to a congregation of armed men. But then, other household slaves had not only refused to join the rebel band but had even protected their masters and their masters' families with arms.[14]

The first element of the militia to reach the field where the slaves had gathered was the Willtown contingent. William Stephens gave

13. Alexander Hewatt, *An Historical Account of the Rise and Progress of the Colonies of South Carolina and Georgia* (London: Donaldson, 1779), 2:73. John Bee, grants recorded in 1704–1731, Series 213019, vols. 38 and 39, SCDAH; A. S. Salley Jr., "Hugh Hext and Some of His Descendants," *South Carolina Historical and Genealogical Magazine* 6 (1905), 31. One should not trust online genealogies, but when they correspond to historical records, they are worth something. See John Bee genealogy, www.e-familytree.net/F208/F208413.htm and www.lynx2ulster.com/ScotchIrishPioneers/015.php.

14. Henry A. M. Smith, "Willtown or New London," *South Carolina Historical and Genealogical Magazine* 10 (1909), 28.

the number of Willtown militiamen at twenty—"The militia was raised upon them throughout the whole province, a party of whom, of about twenty, had met and engaged ninety of them in one body, of whom they had taken four prisoners, and killed ten, and etc." Guided by the sound of singing and music, this party of militia would have had little trouble finding the rebels. They did not know how many slaves they faced, so the men dismounted, loaded their muskets, and approached the clearing cautiously.[15]

The Willtown men were soon reinforced by militia from other parishes and towns: "One hundred planters who had assembled themselves together pursued [the rebels] and found them in an open field where they were dancing, being most of them drunk with the liquors they found in the stores." The militiamen now equaled the rebels in number, but one cannot assume that the militiamen were any better prepared or motivated for pitched battle than the slaves. Militia training in the colonies amounted to little more than periodic musters to parade, check and fire weapons, elect officers, and then retire to the local tavern to drink, tell stories, and some-times engage in fisticuffs. Not all the militia were men of substance. Sons, servants, and laborers served in the militia.[16]

---

15. William Stephens, "The Journal of William Stephens," *Colonial Records of the State of Georgia*, ed. Allen D. Candler (Atlanta: Franklin, 1906), 4:412–413.

16. "A Ranger's Report of Travels with General Oglethorpe, 1739–1742," *Travels in the American Colonies*, ed. Newton D. Mereness (New York: Macmillan, 1916), 222–223. On the militia and slavery, see Sally E. Hadden, *Slave Patrols: Law and Violence in Virginia and the Carolinas* (Cambridge, Mass.: Harvard University Press, 2001), 17–21; on militia preparedness in general, see Michael Bellesiles, *Arming America* (New York: Knopf, 2000), 93–103.

Crouching at the edge of the clearing, the militiamen may have thought to themselves that the slaves' attention span was not up to the mark. They did not seem aware of the approaching danger, and sang and danced as if nothing were wrong. For the slaves, however, singing and dancing was preparation for battle. Communal male song and dance in parts of West Africa was a form of martial art. One after another of the men sang stories of bravery and cleverness in battle. Dance, too, readied the spirit for combat, the movements mimicking

Parker's Ferry Road, between Willtown and U.S. 17 (photograph by author).

the cut and parry of the sword or spear wielder, and of hand-to-hand combat.[17]

The real rebels must have been bone tired, and in their weariness and perhaps in their drunkenness as well, were not as vigilant as they should have been. Still, the slaves would have posted some lookouts, if only to help stragglers find the main body of rebels. These lookouts, if spotting the militia arriving, would have warned the leaders of the rebel band. Apparently, the rebels did not see the militiamen. One possible reason is that the militia came from the direction in which the slaves were marching, not from the road behind them. The most direct route from Willtown to Pon Pon Road was along the east side of the Edisto, up Parker's Ferry Road, and that route would have intersected Pon Pon Road to the south and west of the field where the rebels had paused their march. If the rebels failed to post a watch on the road ahead of them, the militia could have approached unnoticed.

The militia rose up and formed a ragged firing line, much as they had practiced on muster days, and much as a European

17. John K. Thornton, *Africa and Africans in the Making of the Atlantic World, 1400–1800*, 2nd ed. (Cambridge, U.K.: Cambridge University Press, 1998), 239–247; Thornton, "African Dimensions of the Stono Rebellion," *American Historical Review* 96 (October 1991), 1101–1113. There were many such self-defense and attack systems, some involving sticks or other implements. Kilindi Iyi interview, 2004, ejmas.com/jalt/2004jalt/jcsart_green_1104.html; on the dance and martial arts, see Richard Cullen Rath, *How Early America Sounded* (Ithaca, N.Y.: Cornell University Press, 2004), 68–70.

regular force might stand, and fired volleys into the clearing. Officers such as Bee, chosen by the men, stood to the side of the firing line, offering encouragement. Some of the slaves returned the fire, and fell wounded or dead: "[Others,] as soon as they saw their masters...made off as fast as they could to a thicket of woods, excepting one Negroe fellow, who came up to his master. His master asked him if he wanted to kill him. The Negroe answered he did, at the same time snapping a pistol at him, but it misfired and his master shot him through the head."[18]

The story of the bold slave was told to a Georgia ranger by a slave. The tale is eerily similar to an oral tradition from the Bamana Segu at war, a Niger kingdom struggling against Muslim forces: "In the middle of a fight, how to tell friend from enemy: seize him by the shirt and ask, Eh, elder brother, are you one of us?" Storytelling was an important feature of African oral culture. One should not dismiss the slave's account entirely, for the point of stories in the African folk tradition was not to be scientifically objective, to report facts without bias, but to teach lessons. The story is "a directly engaged commentary on how things are or should be; rather than just imitation, they heighten and intensify humanity's most important concerns." For the African in America, slavery taught the necessity of concealing feelings of anger and despair. The trickster figure, common to many folk traditions, could become the slave himself. The trickster could fool a stronger opponent, using wiles and guile to outwit sheer (immoral) force the same way that Brer

18. "A Ranger's Report of Travels with General Oglethorpe, 1739–1742," 223.

Rabbit outwitted the stronger Brer Fox and Brer Bear in the "Uncle Remus" tales.[19]

What the slave–informant knew, either because he was there or because he heard it from slaves who were there, was that a slave braved the musketry, approached a militiaman, and aimed a pistol, which misfired. The words the master spoke and the slave's reply were probably fabrications, but they were not unrealistic inventions. The militiaman, very unlikely to be the rebel's own master, was asking if the slaves wanted to kill their masters. The slave answered that they did. Telling this to the ranger was passing on a message from every slave. However obedient and docile and loyal they might seem, they did not accept slavery and never would.

In the battle, according to Bull, "about 40 Negroes were killed." That figure requires some analysis. The militiamen did not kill forty slaves with their first volley. Muskets are not accurate beyond thirty to forty yards, and the slaves were too spread out to kill so many at one time. An anonymous report sent by a Charles Town merchant to a Boston newspaper revealed: "We...brought down 14 on the spot" and "pursuing them, within two days [we] killed twenty odd more, A number came in and were seized and discharged, and some are yet out, but we hope will soon be taken."

---

19. David Conrad, ed., *A State of Intrigue: The Epic of Bamana Segu according to Tayiru Banbera* (Oxford: Oxford University Press, 1990), 48; Roger D. Abrahams, ed., *African Folktales: Traditional Stories of the Black World* (New York: Pantheon, 1983), 9; Charles Joyner, *Down by the Riverside: A South Carolina Slave Community* (Urbana: University of Illinois Press, 1984), 174. For Uncle Remus (the alter ego of the Georgia folklorist Joel Chandler Harris), see Walter M. Brasch, *Brer Rabbit, Uncle Remus, and the "Cornfield Journalist": The Tale of Joel Chandler Harris* (Macon, Ga.: Mercer University Press, 2000). Of course, these tales came later.

Some were undoubtedly wounded, and the militia killed them where they had fallen. Others were killed where they hid or as they ran. The ranger traveling with Oglethorpe reported: "Many ran back to their plantations thinking they had not been missed, but they were there taken and shot, such as were taken in the field also, were after being examined, shot on the spot, and this to be said to the honor of the Carolina planters, they, notwithstanding the provocation they had received from so many murders, they did not torture one Negro, but only put them to an easy death." In fact, the easy death was not a quick one—the Boston paper reported that "some [slaves were] hanged, and some gibbeted alive."[20]

A few of the rebels retreated in an orderly fashion. It was customary in African infantry warfare for soldiers to mount a fighting retreat, as one might glean from this account: "About 30 escaped from the fight, of whom ten marched about 30 miles southward, and being overtaken by the planters on horseback, fought stoutly for some time and were all killed on the spot." These were quite likely the Angolan soldiers. They stayed together, covered many miles on foot, fought together, and did not run or surrender. "The rest" were "untaken" that day."[21]

Many slaves who for one reason or another were present at the field or followed the marchers returned to their homes. Planters knew from other slaves who was mysteriously missing in the early

20. William Bull to the Board of Trade, October 5, 1739; "An Account of the Negroe Insurrection in South Carolina," 236; "A Letter from South Carolina," *Boston Weekly News-Letter*, November 8, 1739; "A Ranger's Report of Travels with General Oglethorpe, 1739–1742," 222.

21. "An Account of the Negroe Insurrection in South Carolina."

morning hours. These absentees were examined and executed on the spot or excused. According to Oglethorpe, "All that proved to be forced [to join the march] and were not concerned in the murders and burnings were pardoned."[22]

With the remaining rebels still at large and being pursued by the militia, rangers from Georgia, local Indians hired for the purpose, and trusted slaves, the whites began to think about the meaning of the uprising. Robert Pringle, a Charles Town merchant, saw the events in the context of the coming war with Spain. He lived in the city, and his greatest fear was an invasion by sea from Florida or Spain. On September 26, 1739, he wrote to another merchant, John Richards, "I hope our government will order effectual methods for the taking of St. Augustine from the Spaniards which is now become a great detriment to this province by the encouragement and protection given by them to our Negroes that run away there. An insurrection has been made of late here in the country by some Negroes in order to their going there and in less than twenty-four hours they murdered in their way there between twenty and thirty white people and burnt several houses before they were overtaken, though now most of the gang are already taken or cut to pieces." In relating the news to his business associate, Pringle indicated he did not want his business relations interrupted by fears of a general slave uprising.[23]

22. "An Account of the Negroe Insurrection in South Carolina."

23. Robert Pringle to John Richards, September 26, 1739, in *The Letterbook of Robert Pringle*, ed. Walter B. Edgar (Columbia: University of South Carolina Press, 1972), 1:135.

In Ebenezer, Georgia, a Lutheran minister named John Martin Bolzius took a different view of the situation. German Lutherans expelled from Salzburg lived and worshiped in Ebenezer, and he, along with his flock, opposed slavery. He was not a believer in racial equality by any means, but he saw slavery as a peril to whites. He wrote in his diary on Friday, September 28, 1739, "A man brought the news that the Negroes or Moorish slaves are not yet pacified but are roaming around in gangs in the Carolina forests and that ten of them had come as far as the border of this country just two days ago." Bolzius used the same term for the band as Pringle—gangs—implying that the slaves were criminals bent on crime rather than rebels bent on insurrection, and giving a subtle reminder that slavery itself was a crime. The connection between slavery and crime was uppermost on Bolzius's mind as he continued, "In answer to the request of the inhabitants of Savannah to use Moorish slaves for their work, the Lords Trustees have given the simple negative answer that they will never permit a single black to come into the country, for which they have sufficient grounds that they aim at the happiness of the subjects. Mr. Oglethorpe told us here that the misfortune with the negro rebellion had begun on the day of the Lord, which the slaves must desecrate with work and in other ways at the desire, command, and compulsion of their masters." For Bolzius the desecration of the Lord's Sabbath that slavery routinely brought was an offense against God, and the slave rebellion punished that offense.[24]

24. Johann Martin Bolzius, entry for September 28, 1739, *Detailed Reports on the Salzburger Emigrants Who Sailed to America*, ed. Samuel Urlsperger; ed. with an introd. by George Fenwick Jones, trans. Hermann J. Lacher (Athens: University of Georgia Press, 1981), 6:226.

The rebellion was over. The mortal wound had come in the field along the King's Highway, but its last death throes took months, as a mixed force of local Indians, militiamen, trusted slaves, and forest rangers sought out the remaining rebels. The pursuers were compensated for their efforts by the assembly, for when it resumed its interrupted session, in November 1739, Stono was at the top of its agenda.

Nerves remained jangled along the Stono in the months after the rebellion, for a few slaves involved in the uprising were still at large. Three years later, a Charles Town newspaper editor wrote, "We hear that one of the Ringleaders of the last Negro Insurrection (belonging to Mr. Henry Williamson) was lately seized in C[?] Swamp, by two Negro Fellows that ran away from Mr. Grimke, who brought him to Stono, where he immediately was hanged." Fears were strongest at night, for no planter could sleep in confidence that his own slaves had not sympathized with, or taken an undisclosed part in, the violence. Rumors of slaves committing crimes in various places—rumors that might, in less anxious times, would have almost gone unnoticed in the public consciousness—now sparked calls for renewed patrols and heightened security. "Fatigued and wearied" by the constant alarms, the Stono planters turned to the legislature and demanded that it take action.[25]

A committee "to relieve the people about Stono from the dangers arising from domestic enemies" produced a slate of short- and long-term solutions. One was to induce more white people to come

25. *South-Carolina Gazette*, December 27, 1742; Darold D. Wax, "'The Great Risque We Run': The Aftermath of Slave Rebellion at Stono, 1739–1745," *Journal of Negro History* 67 (Summer 1982), 138.

to South Carolina. Another was a series of enactments to prevent another "unhappy accident" like the one at Stono. Slave owners were ordered to provide one white person for every dozen slaves owned to serve in the militia—redundant it would seem, since the militia already included every able-bodied white man. The same redundant burden was laid on every person who owned more than four thousand acres in the colony. If such residents refused to serve, they were to be fined six pounds colony money per month. Fines would go to pay members of the night patrols.[26]

Fines for failing to provide for what was, in essence, their own protection did not appeal to the planters. It seemed that the burden was thrown back upon their shoulders. Perhaps that is where it should logically have rested, for they were the beneficiaries of slave labor, and they were the ones who demanded more and more slaves. But they wanted more police, the common cry of those in a neighborhood shattered by some horrifying criminal event.

The assembly committee complied, amending its proposal to include a "completely armed" patrol to ride the banks of the Stono every night for the next three months, until all the rebels were captured and punished. The commissioners were once again the first line of administration, and they were to determine where the patrols assembled and what would be their patrol routes. Commanders and their men would ride these beats on horseback, the officers paid fifteen pounds in colony money a month, and the rank and file twelve pounds.[27]

26. Committee report, November 10, 1739, *Journal of the Commons House of Assembly, September 12, 1739–March 26, 1741*, pp. 25–26.

27. Committee report, November 20, 1739, *Journal of the Commons House of Assembly, September 12, 1739–March 26, 1741*, p. 36.

The poorer farmers along the Stono were not reassured. The assembly committee reported that "several have deserted their habitations, with their wives and children, and have been obliged to assemble together in numbers, at particular places, for their better security and defense against those Negroes which were concerned in that insurrection who are not yet taken." Finding lodgings at friends houses or in Charles Town, these whites relived the horrors of the uprising every night.[28]

The legislature also rewarded the slaves who had protected their masters. Foremost among these was Thomas Elliott's July, who had not only protected his master and his family, killing one attacker in the process, but had joined in the hunt for the fugitives. July's reward was his freedom. Furthermore, as an "encouragement to other slaves to follow his example in cases of the like nature," July was to have a entire suit of cloths and a pair of shoes. Most slaves went barefoot in the countryside. A freed man needed shoes (along with paperwork stating he was free, lest someone try to carry him back into slavery). The assembly compensated Elliott by assessing July's worth as one thousand pounds colony money.[29]

Thomas Rose's Wells and the slaves at the Wilkinson, Elliott, Peters, Tucker, and Dandridge plantations had also "behaved well" during the uprising, and were also to be rewarded with "ten pounds in cash" and clothing. Note that cash would be of use

28. Committee report, November 21, 1739, *Journal of the Commons House of Assembly, September 12, 1739–March 26, 1741,* p. 37.
29. Committee report, February 29, 1740, *Journal of the Commons House of Assembly, September 12, 1739–March 26, 1741,* p. 221.

only to a slave permitted to buy goods. Likewise, the slaves of Frederick Grimke, Henry Williamson, and Benjamin Williamson were also rewarded for helping save their masters. Only with the rebels did the contest become purely black versus white.[30]

In December 1742, numbers of slaves volunteered to serve with the land troops defending Georgia against Spanish invasion from Florida and pled for "some small reward for their service." William Bull asked the assembly to vote a subsidy for the slaves, arguing it would be "an encouragement on future occasions, wherein the Negroes may be of great service to the Province." But the assembly replied that such payments would set a bad precedent, and in any case, the war was already "burdensome" to the taxpayers in the colony.[31]

❧

The march down the Pon Pon and the battle in the field reminded the whites that slave rebellion was a very real possibility. Whites' fears would quiet over time, but none could ever fool himself or herself again that slaves were content in their chains. Repressive measures were not the only response, however. Rewards to those slaves who informed on or fought against their rebellious brothers

30. Committee report, February 29, 1740, *Journal of the Commons House of Assembly, September 12, 1739–March 26, 1741*, pp. 63–64. Was this genuine gratitude or a policy of "divide and conquer"? Certainly the enslaved experienced carrots and sticks every day, whether on the plantation or in the city. Every regime of oppression offers both rewards and punishment to the oppressed.

31. William Bull to assembly, November 27, and December 1, 1742, *Journal of the Commons House of Assembly, September 14, 1742–January 27, 1744*, ed. J. H. Easterby (Columbia, S.C., 1954), 81; Assembly reply, December 2, 1742, ibid., 86.

and sisters ensured that slave unity could never be assumed by would-be rebels. Some masters adopted a paternal stance toward their slaves, replacing the stern patriarch with the loving father figure. The result of the rebellion was thus to make the slave–master relationship more complex. Perhaps most important is what the rebellion did not affect. The rebellion did not deter South Carolina planters from adding to the numbers of slaves they owned, nor did the rebellion become a precedent for future slave uprisings. In the end, the assembly concluded that it was an "unhappy accident," not a proof that slavery and slave law had gone astray.[32]

32. Committee report, November 10, 1739, *Journal of the Commons House of Assembly, September 12, 1739–March 26, 1741,* p. 25.

· *Five* ·

NEVER FORGET

❧

The fears of the Stono residents would never be entirely stilled and the colony would never be quite as comfortable with its peculiar institution after the uprising. Two years after the Stono violence, the assembly composed a report on South Carolina's part in the invasion of Spanish Florida. The expedition had not gone well, and Florida remained in Spanish hands, but the assembly had a ready scapegoat: Stono. That "cruel and most barbarous" massacre cost twenty-three innocent white men, women, and children their lives, the lawmakers mourned. The rebellion had been put down only through the "blessing of God," the rebels' own misplaced "confidence" in their "strength from the first success," and the militia's swift action. But that effort had drained the colony of energy that should have gone into the invasion. For the rebels "fought for liberty and life," while the whites fought "for their country and every thing that was dear to them."[1]

---

1. "Report of the Committee Appointed to Enquire into the Causes of the Disappointment of Success in the Late Expedition against St. Augustine," July 1, 1741, *The Colonial Records of South Carolina: Journal of the Commons*

But the memory of Stono among the whites was quickly recast in the face of the necessities of the colonial economy. The master class could not do without slave labor. The laboring classes aspired to be planters. The white city folk depended upon slavery for street cleaning, unloading the ships in the harbor, and bringing fresh vegetables, fish, and game to the markets. If Stono left whites paralyzed with fear, South Carolina's very existence as a colony with a black majority would become untenable.

So the recollection of Stono must be fit into a special mold. The story of the rebellion must be shaped as a warning that nevertheless allowed the business of slave trading to continue as usual. Stono reminded the master class that slaves should be treated with a kind of stern decency but watched even more carefully than previously.

The casting of this mold began in the assembly hall in Charles Town when the lawmakers reassembled in October 1739, a month after the rebellion. They had on their table a draft revision of the black code. Without law, there was no slavery. The existing South Carolina slave code, modeled upon the slave codes of the British West Indian islands, was comprehensive. As in all slave codes, slaves were the subject of the code, but its object was to direct the conduct of the masters and other free persons. For example, the code precisely defined the forms of tickets or passes that slaves had to have to leave the plantation. Obviously, the owner or master drafted the ticket, so these provisions were directed to the masters.

House of Assembly, May 18, 1741–July 10, 1742, ed. J. H. Easterby (Columbia, S.C., 1953), 83.

In the two years prior to the uprising, the assembly had dithered and dickered about revising the code. The original dated to the 1690s, when slaves were a minority of the population. The new bill had thirty-six heads, or topics, many protecting the slaves or ameliorating their condition. Masters were not to employ slaves on the Sabbath except in "works of necessity"; masters who "conveyed away" slaves who were suspected of criminal activity (evidently a common enough practice to warrant explicit condemnation in the new law) were themselves to be fined.[2]

There was a tone to the law that suggested the slaves could not stop themselves from violating it. They were thought to be weak in character and self-control, requiring the ruling class to be firm and watchful. Selling strong spirits to slaves was a crime for whites, but slaves were not punished for consuming the liquor. Persons who leased out their slaves to work as fishermen or porters were fined, but the slaves were not punished. Slaves were compelled to testify against masters who violated the slave laws, admittedly an unlikely prospect, hence more of an admonition to the master than a command to the slave. Finally, the law spelled out "penalties to be inflicted on persons who [did] not give sufficient clothing and provisions to their slaves"; stated that "no person [might] inflict any punishment on a slave extending to life or member [i.e., life and limb] without judgment of the magistrates under severe penalties"; and prohibited "willful murder of slaves under heavier penalties, [with] acts of cruelty not extending to life or member to be punished under severe penalties."[3]

2. "Report of the Committee," *Journal of the Commons House of Assembly, November 10, 1736–June 7, 1739,* December 13, 1737, pp. 362–364.

3. "Report of the Committee," p. 364.

Before the uprising, there was no sense of urgency to the revision project. The assembly journals reported that "the house entered on the debate of the above report paragraph by paragraph." Some were agreed to, some postponed, some, evidently, hotly contested. Slave conspiracies were a subject of some concern, as were prohibitions on leasing slaves to act as fishermen and porters. The assembly finally agreed that masters could lease out the slaves in Charles Town but would have to pay a licensing fee for the practice, which would go to pay the city's watchmen. On January 20, 1738, the assembly reviewed its work and pronounced itself satisfied with the body of the act but not with the relationship between the slave law and the duties that importers paid when they brought slaves into the colony. "A very long debate" ensued, and the question was referred back to the committee that had drafted the revision of the slave laws.[4]

More amendments and more debate followed. Anyone who illegally killed a slave was barred from holding public office, even if the victim was the perpetrator's own slave. The last item was a measure of the act's comprehensiveness: it prohibited slaves from wearing offensive apparel—offensive in the eye of the masters. The upper house then had its say, tinkering some more with the provisions. A compromise session was necessary to iron out the wrinkles.[5]

Stono spurred the legislators to action. On November 30, 1739, the assembly listened as Benjamin Whitaker, recently

4. "Report of the Committee," p. 365; January 20, 1738, p. 397; January 21, 1738, p. 399.
5. "Report of the Committee," January 27, 1738, pp. 429–430; March 6, 1738, pp. 512–513.

appointed chief justice of the colony, read the report of a newly appointed committee on the revised code. The revisions were a response to the rebellion. The committee introduced "a clause to regulate the manner of Negroes working on the high roads, so as to prevent too great a number of them from being suffered to work together at the same place." In addition, provision was to be made "to regulate the time when slaves [could] be kept to work, so as to provide against their being over wrought." Immediately, a spate of amendments came from the floor based on what other assemblymen believed happened at Stono, what they assumed would have forestalled Stono, and what they hoped would prevent another Stono. One amendment required that every group of five slaves or more traveling the roads have white person with them. Someone thought that the cause of the rebellion was not slavery itself, or the importation of Angolan warriors, but overwork. Another legislator was determined that slaves not be taught to write, lest they forge passes for themselves or other slaves.[6]

Although it was not included in the bill, the assembly speaker Charles Pinckney proposed that the lieutenant governor "take all the care in your power to guard against any further wicked designs [the slaves might] have in agitation." In particular, slave gatherings and travel around the countryside, traditional on Christmas Day, were to be closely watched by the militia—a precautionary measure to be funded out of the public treasury. There was, in addition, a ban on slave use or ownership of musical instruments,

6. November 30, 1739, *Journal of the Commons House of Assembly, September 12, 1739–March 26, 1741*, p. 68.

particularly drums, lest they be employed to signal the beginning of an uprising.[7]

The changes in the law did not punish all slaves for the rebellion. Quite the opposite. Some of the provisions of the new law showed a carefully measured leniency, doled out like the suits of clothing distributed to the loyal slaves. So far as the law was concerned, Stono bid the masters hurry their deliberations but did not speed the outcome of those deliberations very much. For after Stono, as before, the relationship between master and slave was a complex interpersonal one.

For some, like Thomas Sacheverell, slaves remained property. He had no interest in individual slaves or their fate. In his will he commended his soul "into the hands of God" and set aside funds for a proper Christian burial. To his wife, Ann, he gave money and a hunting horse, to his daughters and sons he gave land and his slave servant Dinah, with all her future children. But he made no special provisions for any of his other slaves. They were part of the property to be divided among his heirs. Six years before, Stono had terrified and divided his household. He surely remembered it when he wrote his will. But nothing in or about those horrific days changed the way he distributed his slave property.[8]

7. Ibid., p. 69. Slaves' musicality could not be chained in this manner. In response to the ban on instruments, slaves developed body music and used kitchen implements as musical instruments. Hambone music with spoons, or clapping, to keep rhythm, has been dated back to the Stono rebellion.

8. Thomas Sacheverell, will, December 22, 1742, will book, 1740–1747, p. 476, South Carolina Department of Archives and History [SCDAH], Columbia, S.C.

Alexander Hext's slaves had played multiple roles in the rebellion. Across his lands in St. Johns, St. Pauls, and elsewhere in Colleton; on his estate in Berkeley County; and in his townhouse in Charles Town, his more than ninety enslaved men and women knew firsthand, or soon learned, what had occurred along King's Highway. Though he knew every one of his slaves by name, when he came near death he divided them up among his heirs, along with his lands, boats, canoes, carts, wagons, carriages, horses, hogs, cattle, furniture, plate, jewels, and "household stuff."[9]

Royal Sprye remembered his wife and friends in his will, a proof of the importance of family among the planters and of the precariousness of life in the colony. Mary Sprye was to retain control over everything she brought into the marriage. She also had dower rights to one-third of the rest of the estate, and the right to remain in the plantation house during her life. She could not sell or otherwise dispose of the house or the lands, however, or the two household slaves, Scipio and Dilly, both children. The estate that remained went to Sprye's son and daughter. For that purpose, Sprye listed just about every one of his possessions, including the honey from his bees and the dairy from his cattle. Everything went somewhere, every slave, every horse, everything.

To his "trusty friends" John Bee and Thomas Sacheverell, Sprye gave four slaves, a portion of their labor to be spent on salary for a minister in St. John's Episcopal Church. In effect, even after his death he would be the master of all he surveyed, determining who got what. Sprye did not mention the servants he lost

9. Alexander Hext, will, July 9, 1741, will book, 1740–1741, p. 32, SCDAH.

when the rebels burned his house and killed everyone they could find in it. They were replaceable.[10]

Thomas Rose alone among the planters referred to the rebellion explicitly in later days. But even he refused to dwell on the terror. Instead, he selectively recalled the loyalty of a slave, writing, "And whereas my Negro fellow Wells has faithfully and honestly demeaned himself in consideration whereof and for other good services done and performed I will and direct he shall take care of my cow pen reserving to him a liberty of choice to fix upon any of my plantation and shall remain upon such place he pleased." Wells was to be paid the "sum of fifty pounds current money every year during the term of . . . twelve years," after which he was to be free "of servitude." Wells was the slave who had hidden Rose and his family from the incendiaries, and this was his reward. Rose also provided that his old slaves John, Pendar, and Charles were to be kept within the family and treated with loving care. Indeed, insofar as he could from beyond the grave, Rose wanted his slaves treated decently, for he owed them much.[11]

So long as slavery existed, the memory of Stono could not be lost among the white population. Surely no one in power forgot the lessons of Stono. Efforts to strengthen the patrols and the militia echoed their initial failures during the Stono uprising. But that memory had a sharply divided quality. On the one hand, slavery posed mortal dangers to the planters every day, to which

10. Royal Sprye, will, December 17, 1746, will book, 1740–1746, p. 614, SCDAH.
11. Thomas Rose, will, May 25, 1756, will book, 1752–1756, p. 518, SCDAH.

they responded with calls for increased vigilance. Periodically, rumors of a slave plot burst into flame, and suspected plotters were rounded up and interrogated, with corporal punishment often used to induce confessions or elicit accusations against other slaves. In 1759 two free blacks and one slave were charged with attempting to raise a rebellion, the sort of charge that was hard to prove but all too easy to believe. Six years later, during the protests against the Stamp Act in Charles Town accusing the imperial government of enslaving the planters, another group of enslaved men was punished for contemplating their own protest against slavery. On the eve of the American Revolution, the free black Thomas Jeremiah was accused of plotting rebellion, and even the strenuous efforts of the royal governor could not save Jeremiah from the noose.[12]

On the other hand, during the American Revolution, a few South Carolinians saw slavery as a danger to the state. For some whites, Stono served as an object lesson of the poisoned fruits of one man owning another. Alexander Hewatt believed that "upon the slightest reflection all men must confess that those Africans, whom the powers of Europe have conspired to enslave, are by nature equally free and independent...as Europeans themselves." The indignities and cruelties of the middle passage, the incidental

12. J. William Harris, *The Hanging of Thomas Jeremiah: A Free Black Man's Encounter with Liberty* (New Haven, Conn.: Yale University Press, 2010), cited with permission of the author; Philip Morgan, *Slave Counterpoint: Black Culture in the Eighteenth-Century Chesapeake and Low Country* (Chapel Hill: University of North Carolina Press, 1998), 648–649; Sylvia Frey, *Water from the Rock: Black Resistance in a Revolutionary Age* (Princeton: Princeton University Press, 1991), 16.

and intentional hardships inflicted on them in a land so distant from their own by a people so foreign to them, might naturally lead them to rebel. The laws and the usages of the colony might give to the master "absolute property" in the slave, but the slaves remained human and even the "severest penalties" for the mere contemplation of freedom could not suppress their desire for liberty. If, "in justice to the planters of Carolina," they treated their slaves far better than did their counterparts in the Caribbean, "cruelty and negligence always accompanied slavery." Thus "doomed to endless labor," the slaves at Stono "assembled, elected a captain, and rose up in rebellion."[13]

But without slavery the new state could not prosper, as most among the master class conceded. Though a "state of constant fear" might be felt by the whites, it had to be quarantined. The Stono rebels were not typical of the slaves. Indeed, they "compelled the Negroes to join them." Though the white womenfolk were "trembling," the men bravely set out and crushed the rebel band. From Stono, slaves had learned how futile rebellion was.[14]

Antebellum white South Carolina created a template for Stono, a rigid, single-minded narrative that explained the rebellion while justifying slavery. William Gilmore Simms, whose proslavery views colored his essays and his fictional works, judged that "runaways, seduced from their masters by the Spanish ... who

13. Alexander Hewatt, *An Historical Account of the Rise and Progress of the Colonies of South Carolina and Georgia* (London: Donaldson, 1779), 2:92–97, 105, 72.

14. David Ramsay, *History of South Carolina from Its First Settlement in 1670 to the Year 1808* (Newberry, S.C.: W. J. Duffie, 1858), 62.

rose in revolt upon the Stono, and having plundered some store-houses of their arms and ammunition, elected a captain and proceeded with drums and colors." Bee acted the part of a Francis Marion or other revolutionary war hero, dividing his force and attacking from the front with one portion of the men, while dispatching a second troop to close off avenues of escape. The rebel leaders were executed, but "the greater number," having returned with due contrition to their plantation homes, "were received to mercy." There was no terror, nor confusion on the part of the whites, and the greatest number of the blacks showed that slavery was their natural estate. After all, as William Johnson wrote in 1822, "There exists nothing of that personal hostility between the master and slave, that theorists suppose must be the result of the relation they bear to each other."[15]

Although Stono could not be ignored (much less forgotten), white polite conversation avoided the topic. A foreign visitor to the United States, not bound by the unwritten conventions of the slave South, recognized a conspiracy of silence among the whites as broad as the much-feared conspiracy among the slaves. Alexis de Tocqueville visited South Carolina, among other slave states, in 1833. In his *Democracy in America* (1835) he wrote of the dangers of slave uprisings: "In the southern states there is a silence; one avoids discussing it with one's friends, each man…hides it from himself.[16]

15. William Gilmore Simms, *The History of South Carolina* (Charleston: Babcock, 1840), 107–108; William Johnson, *Sketches of the Life and Correspondence of Nathanael Greene* (Charleston, S.C.: n.p., 1822), 2:347.

16. Alexis de Tocqueville, *Democracy in America* [1837] (repr., New York: Doubleday, 1960), 358.

The abolitionists were not so reticent about the uprising, seeing it as a warning and a proof of the inhumanity of slavery. In the *Liberty Bell*, Maria Chapman's annual Boston abolitionist miscellany, Edmund Quincy, a Massachusetts abolitionist from one of Boston's foremost families, contrived an antislavery short story, which tells of a meeting on the eve of the American Revolution, when a Mr. Langdon from Massachusetts traveled to the colonial South Carolina plantation of Mount Verney, owned by Mr. Verney. The lush greenery, the hospitality of the planter, the curiosity of the simple but good-hearted Negroes, Langdon reported, was a staple of antebellum travel narratives. After a delightful and filling repast, Langdon and Verney turned to serious topics of discussion among gentlemen. The planter revealed that, should conflict with England come, the slaves would be a fifth column within the colony, informing the British of colonial preparations and turning on their masters when the opportunity arose. The slaves had no sentimental attachment to their masters, Verney insisted, for as a child the planter had been the only one of his family to survive the massacre at Stono. Langdon learned that Verney's father's longtime body servant, a slave named Arnold, had conceived and nurtured a plan for freeing his brothers and sisters. He chose the moment when war with Spanish Florida loomed and plotted the extermination of the whites. Arnold truly loved his master's children, including the narrator of the tale, and he wept at the prospect of causing their deaths, but in the end the suffering of his race won out over his personal attachments. He organized and led the rebellion of slaves on his and nearby plantations. They marched to Stono, a settlement, to seize the arms and ammunition in a warehouse, and, numbering five hundred, marched to glory and death.

Although the specifics are not quite right—Quincy had not done any research of his own (there was no settlement named Stono, the only armory in the colony was in Charles Town, and the rebel band was only one-fifth as large as he made it)—the story was not pure invention. Alexander Hewatt's or David Ramsay's histories could have been its source; Nat Turner's rebellion was obviously its inspiration. Perhaps—only perhaps—Quincy also had an informant or informants who told him what they had heard from their elders who were alive at the time. Quincy's account of what Arnold was thinking might not then have been pure abolitionist pamphleteering, though its message ran all through abolitionist writing—even slaveholders who thought themselves genteel and kindly could not forever escape the fate of Verney's family. Indeed, when he learned of Verney's experience, Langdon urged the planter to civilize and free the slaves, but Verney moaned that he had the wolf by the ears, and could not let him go.[17]

As the Civil War approached, antebellum Southern political leaders argued long and loud that abolitionists' attacks on slavery, stirring up memories of Stono, would lead to massive slave revolts. As the December 24, 1860, South Carolina Declaration of the Causes of Secession explained, "[Northern states had] denounced as sinful the institution of slavery [and] permitted open establishment among them of societies, whose avowed object [was] to disturb the peace and to eloign [carry away and hide] the property of the citi-

17. Edmund Quincy, "Mount Verney: Or, An Incident of Insurrection," *Liberty Bell* 8 (1847), 165–228. On Chapman and *Liberty Bell*, see Debra Gold Hansen, *Strained Sisterhood: Gender and Class in the Boston Female Anti-slavery Society* (Amherst: University of Massachusetts Press, 1993), 134–135.

zens of other States. They [had] encouraged and assisted thousands of…slaves to leave their homes; and those who remain[ed], [had] been incited by emissaries, books and pictures to servile insurrection." No such insurrection took place after Stono, as it happened, and only a handful of abolitionists wished to see one.

With slavery ended by the Thirteenth Amendment and the defeat of the Confederacy in 1865, silence once again descended on Stono. It was as if there were a tacit consensus not to mention the rebellion in South Carolina. Typically, W. Roy Smith's 1903 *South Carolina as a Royal Province, 1719–1779* cited Stono only 6 times in more than 420 pages of text and never actually described the event. Stono had merely been the occasion for legislative reform of the slave code. From 1900 to 1951, the *South Carolina Historical and Genealogical Magazine*, the forerunner of the *South Carolina Historical Magazine*, did not discuss the revolt. The bated silence imposed by the white survivors on themselves became an incurious absentmindedness in their distant descendants.

Black memory of the events was clear in the years following the rebellion. The slaves who returned from Hutchenson's, the slaves who watched the armed band's progress down the Pon Pon, the slaves who danced and sang but departed the field before the arrival of the militia—surely they remembered everything, even if they played dumb when later questioned about the events. In later years, slave exhorters, lay preachers melding the traditions of African religion with Christianity, told gatherings of slaves that they would be delivered from bondage just like the Israelites in Egypt. The overtones of Stono surely gave special meaning to these hymns.[18]

18. Morgan, *Slave Counterpoint*, 650–651.

But what exactly did the enslaved remember? Likely, there were many memories, and many kinds of memories, among the black people of South Carolina following Stono. For many bondmen and women the story would not have begun where the white accounts began, with the break-in at Hutchenson's store, but with preparation and remonstration in the quarters. These memories would be folded into the actual mayhem, until the seams between them vanished. Prophecies of bloodletting and terror and trusted African methods of telling the future were surely consulted, and would-be rebels would have sought amulets, potions, and powders to make them invisible or impervious to wounds. Whatever plans were made in these days, not all of the planners were with the drainage crew that night. Some of the planners never did participate in the episode. The identities of those who stayed and those who joined in the march would shift and reform in later memory, like the shapes of spirits in the night. Memory would recall the time when some slaves left the quarters to join the march, a time of urgency, of hurried farewells and exhortations to victory. Participants and witnesses shared these memories with a trusted circle of family and friends. Memory fused African stories of military prowess with details of the Stono fight. In time these memories too would become part of a collective set of stories, passed down from generation to generation.[19]

19. See, e.g., the role of "Gullah Jack" in Nat Turner's Virginia rebellion; Kenneth S. Greenberg, ed., *The Confessions of Nat Turner* (Boston: Bedford, 1996), 17; Richard Price, *Alabi's World* (Baltimore: Johns Hopkins University Press, 1990), 26–27; Mark P. Leone and Gladys-Marie Fry, "Conjuring in the Big House Kitchen: An Interpretation of African America Belief Systems Based on the Uses of Archeology and Folklore Sources," *Journal of American Folklore* 112 (1999), 372–403.

The prolonged pursuit of the surviving rebels hints that some of the men visited their old haunts before they were captured or finally escaped. Perhaps their stories of short-lived freedom inspired other slaves to plan for the comprehensive uprising the Stono band failed to raise. It is entirely possible that the next year's rumored rebellions, in Goose Creek, north of the Stono, and later in Charles Town, were the result of Stono. Certainly the response of authorities was colored by Stono. In Charles Town, a year after Stono, sixty-seven slaves were brought to trial and two dozen were hanged.[20]

A conspiracy was easy to prove—a few slaves talking about rebelling would serve. Conspiracy was the axle around which slave criminal law turned, for a slave conspiracy was defined as two or more bondmen talking about crime. An actual rebellion was far harder to mount. Some much-storied slave rebellions, such as Denmark Vesey's alleged rebellion in Charles Town, in 1821–1822, were no more than unfulfilled conspiracies. Or perhaps there had been no conspiracy at all at Goose Creek and Charles Town in 1740, merely the overwrought imagination of whites adding detail to gossip.[21]

There was an almost eerie similarity between the Stono rebellion and the Nat Turner uprising in Southampton County, Virginia, in the late summer of 1831. There, a self-taught prophet

20. Herbert Aptheker, *American Negro Slave Revolts* (New York: International, 1943), 189, gives a much larger figure, but Robert Olwell, *Masters, Slaves, and Subjects*, 26, offers the more accurate figures above.

21. Douglas R. Egerton, *He Shall Go out Free: The Lives of Denmark Vesey* (Madison, Wisc.: Madison House, 1999), 132; Michael P. Johnson, "Denmark Vesey and His Co-Conspirators," *William and Mary Quarterly*, 3rd ser., 58 (October 2001), 916 and after.

and mystic led a small band of male slaves that grew as night turned to day. They marched from house to house and killed everyone they found, regardless of age or sex. By midmorning, word had spread of the rising, and the militia confronted the rebel band, killing all but a few. They tried to hide and were captured. Turner was tried by a court of law and condemned, after giving an account of his life that was later published.

What memories did the slaves of Southampton County retain of those days? What memories did they pass on? Memory was free to rewrite events, to reimagine them, to use them. James McGee was a very special custodian of such memories, in fact the self-appointed guardian of the memory of Nat Turner. McGee was not a journalist, a teacher, or a historian, but a living treasury of oral and folk tales, gathering and refashioning what generations of black folks heard and saw and then retold of the Turner rebellion. He privileged the oral, the recollected, over the written document, and private accounts passed down over the years over public accounts published at the time. By so doing, he gleaned and surmised the context and meaning of events from the rebel side in ways that officials and scholars might miss. And what emerged from this exercise in collective recollection was the collective pride in the courage of the rebels, even among those who refused to join Turner.[22]

For pride, anger, and caution mixed all together must have become part of the black folk memory of Stono. Such memory sometimes plays tricks, but the tricks all have a function. The actual event is less important than its social meaning; the moral drawn

22. Kenneth S. Greenberg, "Name, Face, Body," in *Nat Turner: A Slave Rebellion in History and Memory*, ed. Kenneth S. Greenberg (New York: Oxford University Press, 2003), 17–18.

from the story and characters serves a purpose that the actual details may cloud or even refute. What David Blight has called "the music of words" enhanced and enlivened "moral indictments." The Works Progress Administration's Federal Writers Program underwrote interviews with survivors of slavery in the middle 1930s. In it one finds the one recorded direct echo of Stono. One elderly freedman told a WPA oral historian, "My granddaddy was a son of the son of the Stono slave commander. He say his daddy often take him over de route of de rebel slave march, dat time when dere was sho' big trouble all 'bout dat neighborhood." Cato, the elected leader, was "teached how to read and write by his rich master." He could command, and slaves "much 'bused by dere masters" joined him. The slaves "work fast, covin' 15 miles, passin' many fine plantations....dey they take what they want." And when they faced the militia, they "stand their ground."[23]

George Cato's account is a curious mixture of folk memory, wishful thinking, black pride, and knowledge of the textual sources. For he also told Bull's story and the militia story, things that his grandfather could not have heard from oral accounts. Thus, memory, in time, merged what descendants of both whites and blacks recalled, what was oral and what was written. Just as Stono belonged to the history of all South Carolinians, so, too, did its memory.

❧

In the Civil Rights era, historians rediscovered these many visions of Stono and gave them new life. Herbert Aptheker's series of

---

23. David W. Blight, *Beyond the Battlefield: Race, Memory, and the American Civil War* (Amherst: University of Massachusetts Press, 2002), 23; Cato, "The Stono Insurrection Described by a Descendant of the Leader," *The American Slave*, supplement, series 1, 11:98–100.

books on slave uprisings, first published in 1939, recalled the importance of Stono. Peter Wood's prize-winning *Black Majority* (1974), closed with an entire chapter on Stono, for him an object lesson on the wages of oppression. As he noted, Stono was "preceded by a series of projected insurrections, any one of which could have assumed significant proportions." The Africanist John Thornton's provocative *American Historical Review* (1991) relocated Stono in the traditions of African warfare, reminding scholars and students of U.S. history to appreciate "the African roots of the Stono rebellion." Mark Smith's thoughtful piece in the *Journal of Southern History* (2001) teased out Christian themes in the uprising, which he argued "highlights the importance of the rebels' memories of Catholicism generally and of the Kongolese veneration of the Virgin Mary specifically." Smith's later collection on Stono collated primary and secondary sources. Philip Morgan's magisterial *Slave Counterpoint* set Stono in its proper context, the anxious ongoing story of slavery. Stono is now a topic in every college U.S. history survey textbook. What was lost has been found.[24]

24. Peter Wood, *Black Majority: Negroes in Colonial South Carolina through the Stono Rebellion* (New York: Norton, 1973), 308–309; John Thornton, "African Dimensions of the Stono Rebellion," *American Historical Review* 96 (October 1991), 1102; Mark Smith, "Remembering Mary, Shaping Revolt: Reconsidering the Stono Rebellion," *Journal of Southern History* 67 (2001)," 513; in textbooks, see, e.g., David Goldfield et al., *The American Journey: A History of the United States* (Saddle Brook, N.J.: Prentice Hall, 1998), 1:81; Eric Foner, *Give Me Liberty! An American History*, 2nd ed. (New York: Norton, 2008), 1:139; and James L. Roark et al., *The American Promise: A History of the United States*, 3rd ed. (Boston: Bedford, 2006), 1:153.

Epilogue

MEANINGS

WHAT DID THE INCIDENT AT STONO MEAN TO THE PEOPLE who lived through it? What did it tell them about their world? How did Stono change that world? What does the incident tell us about our history? Why is it important to remember what happened that day?

For the scholar and the student of history, "important" can have two quite different kinds of significance. An event may be important because it reveals the inner workings of a time and place. It reflects and magnifies, so that we can see into actions and words. An event also may be important because of its effect on later events. That is, an event may be an important cause of future changes. Stono is important for the first reason, not the second. It did not change slavery in practice or in theory. It did not shake the determination of South Carolina's master class to retain slavery. Although Stono, the war with Spain, and a higher import duty on slaves for a time retarded the importation of slaves, in the years between 1739 and the end of the overseas slave trade in 1808, planters invested more and more of their capital in slave labor.

By examining Stono, we can peer into the heart of darkness that was human bondage—and discover how that dark heart beat throughout our early history. It is said that history teaches lessons, and those who ignore the lessons are fated to suffer for their negligence. There are many among us, including our political leaders, our educators, and our community spokespeople, who regard our history first and foremost as a subject of heroic deeds and noble ideals. The study of history, in their view, should inspire unity, pride, and celebration. For some, this "traditional" history is a necessary component of patriotism. In it, the dates and places remembered in historical celebrations are the founding of the nation and its victories in wars. Ordinary working people are the designated audiences for this history, not its subject.

The episode at Stono challenges all of these assumptions. Its chief actors are not heroes. Nor are they famous. Its significance is not a cause for celebration. Inhumanity in the name of exploitation of people for profit is as much a theme in our history as democracy, progress, and opportunity. Stono was not the exception to the rule of progress, equality, and opportunity, though there were few genuine slave rebellions in those days. Instead, it was the natural outcome of the everyday deformities of slavery and the staple-crop enterprise that demanded slave labor.

The law, too, was deformed by these constraints. We are proud that we are a people of laws, and proclaim to the world the achievements of our constitutions. But law at Stono deformed all the normal relationships among people according to vicious racial distinctions. It forced one people to labor for another in perpetuity. It punished the quest for freedom and denied equality on racial grounds. And when the slaves at Stono were rounded up and executed or spared, according to the individual judgments of the militia and the masters, the law was not even consulted. All judgments were summary.

But that was then. What has Stono to teach us today? We no longer allow people to be regarded as property or to be owned by other people. According to the tenet in the philosophy of history called historical-mindedness, we must view Stono in the light of its time, and not our own. Then, slavery existed throughout the world. Indeed, in many countries it was the hallmark or the price of economic progress. Stono continued to have different meanings to different people, according to the time in which they lived. That is why South Carolina historians ignored it during the Jim Crow years, and why, by contrast, it became so important to historians during the civil rights era.

But before we decide that the message depends upon who is listening, there are certain lessons that apply to us all. The first is the lesson that underlies my attempt to make sense of the events at Stono even though little primary source material survives. I assumed that the slaves, the masters, the militia, and the lawgivers were not fundamentally different from us. Their world was different, but human vices and virtues have not changed that much. Some slaves were bold, some timid; some risked all, while some preferred to avoid risk. Some were loyal to their masters, some indifferent, some deeply hostile. Some masters were almost embarrassed to be so heavily dependent on African labor. Some saw themselves as benevolent patriarchs. Some were disfigured by their avarice and cynical cruelty. Some were pious Christians, while others only pretended to be pious. It is only by assuming this similarity of emotion and thought process across time that can we see the lessons in history at all.

Tempt people to enslave others with promises of great riches, and scruples will give way to rationalizations. Drive people too far, and they will react violently. Ignore the uniqueness of each person, and personal uniqueness will dissolve into the harshness of stereotyping and discrimination. By contrast, treat individuals according to their deserts and they will return extraordinary loyalty and kindness.

Many years ago, an older colleague overheard me teaching these lessons in an early U.S. history survey course. He gently chided me that I was not historical-minded enough. I was reading our preferences for human dignity back into a time when servitude of all kinds was normal and no one was a democrat, much less a believer in the equality of the races. My response then I still affirm. Then, as now, all believe in their own dignity and all own a sense of their own worth. In every colony, servants went to court to complain of their masters' mistreatment. Slaves simply lacked the legal identity to do likewise. But complain they did, by running away, by talking back, by slowing down at work, by making up stories and songs that censured their masters, and in a thousand other ways short of rebellion. Everything may have changed since then, but nothing has really changed when it comes to treating others as we would like to be treated ourselves. When this golden rule was discarded, Stono and its like became inevitable.

A second lesson is quite opposite the golden rule and just as important. Every society has within itself the means of oppression. Even a democratic republic under a constitution of laws like our own may reach into this store of repressive measures when danger threatens. The refusal of government to protect its most vulnerable citizens—the poor, the immigrant, the despised minority—is a kind of oppression. The positive use by government of courts to oppress those who dissent represents a kindred form of tyranny. Stono evidenced both the negative and the positive forms of oppression. The authorities were supposed to intervene to stay the hand of brutal masters but did not. The authorities did clamp down on anyone who objected to the institution of slavery, however.

The same atavistic impulse to stigmatize people simply because of their ethnicity or religion, along with a willingness to break the law or use the law to quell dissent, has been a characteristic of modern democratic governments. When such governments, including our own, feel themselves under assault, they react much as the South Carolina government did during and after Stono. They curb civil rights, intrude into private lives, use torture, or impose indefinite incarceration in the name of national security. Behind these illicit measures may be very real fears, the same fears that both slaves and enslavers felt at Stono. And there may be criminals and crimes that need to be punished. But fear should not be an excuse to oppress.

And make no mistake. Oppression works—not forever, not on everyone, but often enough. Knowing this, totalitarian regimes such as Hitler's Nazi Germany and Stalin's Communist Soviet Union imprisoned, tortured, and butchered ethnic minorities and dissenters by the millions. Nothing stopped them until war intervened. The war that erupted between England and Spain in 1739 ended Stono more effectively than any of the repressive measures the government contemplated. Slaves showed their loyalty and their manhood by volunteering to join the forces sent to Georgia, serving alongside the very militiamen who had put down Stono. The same William Bull who demanded that all the rebels be found and executed would three years later publicly argue for rewards for the slaves who served in the war.

Such ironies of time, place, and action ran all though slavery, and this is the last important lesson of Stono for us. History is filled with irony, for our actions rarely result in precisely what we planned. The exertions of the rebels at Stono did not lead to their freedom or to the mitigation of the treatment of their fellow slaves. Violence did not lead to liberation. We, too, need to learn that following our impulses of revenge or our desire for immediate gain through conquest and oppression will not gain for us what we expect. A decent respect for the opinions of mankind, as one slaveholder wrote thirty-seven years after Stono, is a far better guarantor of human liberty than rebellion or repression.

Explanatory Essay

Reading
the Sources on Stono

❦

Historians are artists. They transform the raw material of "primary sources"—contemporary accounts of events, movements, and people—into narratives that we can understand today. They are storytellers who must tell truths, or as much of the truth as the surviving primary sources reveal. But like all documents that people prepare, the primary sources do not speak for themselves, nor do they take us back to the past by themselves. We must "listen" to written documents, hearing the words on the page as if spoken to us by their authors. Even more, we must decode the silences between the words, seeking what their author left out, and why.[1]

Historians are also social scientists. They borrow from the other social sciences, such as anthropology and sociology, to

1. Winthrop D. Jordan, *Tumult and Silence at Second Creek: An Inquiry into a Civil War Slave Conspiracy*, rev. ed. (Baton Rouge: Louisiana State University Press, 1995), 3.

analyze human action and motive. They look for patterns in the evidence and make comparisons across time and place. History is "interdisciplinary," bringing together under one roof all relevant methods of inquiry into the past. Some of these methods involve mental experiments, weighing various possible explanations to approach the truth.

Telling the story of Stono requires both imagination and analysis. Unlike some slave uprisings, which were thoroughly documented in official reports and private correspondence, Stono left behind few primary-source accounts and only one surviving eyewitness account of a portion of the events. Had criminal court records of trials of the rebels and other such legal records been prepared, and survived, we would know much more. But there were no trials of the accused. The absence of detailed accounts from those on the scene and documentary testimony at trial throws us back on the handful of primary sources that did describe the events.

Looking briefly at the most often quoted of the primary sources, one realizes immediately that their authors saw the events through the filter of their own interests and assumptions. Four days after the violence at Stono, William Stephens, an agent for the Georgia proprietors sent to Savannah to watch over their interests, noted in his diary that South Carolina "Negroes had made an insurrection, which began first at Stonoe [sic] (midway between Charles-Town and Port Royal) where they had forced a large store, furnished themselves with arms and ammunition," and then "killed all the family on that plantation, and diverse other white people, burning and destroying all that came in their way, so that the messenger who came, told us the country thereabout was full of flames."[2]

An even more distant account in time and space, from a captain of militia traveling with the Georgia governor James Oglethorpe in the Indian Country on the upper Savannah River, reported "a Negroe came to the General [Oglethorpe] and told him that what was said of the Negroes Rising in Carolina was true and that they had marched to Stono Bridge where they had murdered two storekeepers." The informant continued that the rebels had "cut their heads off and set them on the stairs." No other account mentioned this atrocity, by the way. The captain continued that the rebels also "robbed the stores of what they wanted and went on killing what men, women, and children they met, burning houses and committing other outrages."[3]

Oglethorpe himself reported on the events. The governor was opposed to slavery, insisted that a ban on slavery in Georgia be written into the laws of the colony, and fought those who illegally brought slaves into the colony. As he had noted eight months earlier, when a band of fugitive slaves from South Carolina had crossed his colony on their way to Florida, "if we allow slaves [in Georgia] we act against the very principles by which we associated together, which was to relieve the distressed [in England]." He added, "Whereas, now we should occasion the misery of

2. William Stephens, "The Journal of William Stephens," *Colonial Records of the State of Georgia*, ed. Allen D. Candler (Atlanta: Franklin, 1906) 4:412–413.

3. "A Ranger's Report of Travels with General Oglethorpe, 1739–1742," *Travels in the American Colonies*, ed. Newton D. Mereness (New York: Macmillan, 1916), 222–223.

thousands in Africa, by setting men upon arts to buy and bring into perpetual slavery the poor people who now live free there. Instead of strengthening we should weaken the frontier of America, [and we would] give away to the owners of slavery that land which was designed as a refuge to [the] persecuted."[4]

Clearly, Oglethorpe viewed the rebellion as a good reason not to allow slaves into Georgia, and used his account of the uprising to counter the lobbying of South Carolina masters and their allies in Georgia with the colony's trustees in England. "On the 9th day of September last being Sunday which is the day the planters allow them [i.e., the slaves] to work for themselves," he wrote to Georgia's trustees in England, "some Angola Negroes assembled, to the number of twenty, and one who was called Jemmy was their captain, [and] they surprised a warehouse belonging to Mr. Hutchenson, at a place called Stonehow, they there killed Mr. Robert Bathurst and Mr. Gibbs, plundered the house and took a pretty many small arms and power, which were there for sale."

Oglethorpe assumed the worst—that the slaves had gathered for the purpose of raiding the warehouse. His account stressed the horrors of slave rebellion and implied that such rebellions were inevitable in a colony with slaves. He continued, "Next they plundered and burnt Mr. [...] Godfrey's house, and killed him, his daughter and son. They then turned back and marched southward along Pons Pons," presumably not along the shore of

---

4. Phinizy Spalding, *Oglethorpe in America* (Chicago: University of Chicago Press, 1977), 49–51; James Oglethorpe to the Trustees, January 17, 1739, Mills Lane, ed., *General Oglethorpe's Georgia* (Savannah, Ga.: Beehive, 1975), 2:389.

the South Edisto River, the Indian name for which was Pon Pon, but the "the road from Georgia to Augustine." Then, carrying out what seemed to Oglethorpe to be a proof of the slaves' barbarous and violent nature, "they broke open and plundered Mr. Lemy's house, and killed him, his wife and child."

Supposedly having made a plan, whose purpose was to sow confusion among the whites and raise an army of the blacks, "they marched on" toward the most grisly prospect. Plainly, the very idea that a slave army was advancing toward the Georgia border gravely concerned Oglethorpe, particularly one that "marched on with colors displayed, and two drums beating, pursuing all the white people they met with, and killing man woman and child when they could come up to them."[5]

Governor Bull came upon the rebel band at midmorning, and almost a month later reported what he saw, along with the rest of the day's events, to authorities in England. His account was a day late and a dollar short. What might easily have been the most detailed retelling of the events was instead remarkably brief and general. He blamed the Spanish for inciting the slaves to rebellion, kept his part in the events to a bare minimum, praised the militia for its highly competent crushing of the revolt, and closed with the assertion that the incident was over. With every means at

5. "An Account of the Negroe Insurrection in South Carolina," *Colonial Records of the State of Georgia*, ed. Allen D. Candler, William L. Northern, and Lucian L. Knight (Atlanta: Byrd, 1913) volume 22 (part 2): 232–236. Oglethorpe's identification of Jemmy was repeated in *London Magazine and Monthly Chronologer*, March 1740, p. 152. The magazine's squib had no more authority, of course, than Oglethorpe's secondhand account. Jemmy was not a name mentioned in the legislative accounts of planters seeking compensation for the death of their rebellious slaves.

his disposal to give a thorough account, to interview planters and slaves, to probe the causes and comment on the consequences, he kept his words to a select few. We can only surmise that he was not proud of his flight from the band or his later role in rounding up the remnants of the rebels. For days he must have pondered how to couch his report—for he was the governor-general, charged with keeping order, and he had failed in that duty.[6]

In short, everyone who wrote about Stono interpreted the event in light of his own needs, expectations, desires, and interests. Though all of the primary-source authors intended to be objective (save perhaps Bull—the only eyewitness, as it happened, and the only source who had to protect his own reputation), none of the accounts was literally accurate. The parable of the blind men and the elephant comes to mind. Each touched a different part of the animal, and each reached a different conclusion about what he had touched, based on limited information.

Of the primary sources' authors, Bull alone was present at the uprising. But this did not deter the others from speaking as though they had firsthand knowledge. We may well ask why someone who had only hearsay for a source write with such authority? Why were there no qualifiers or modifiers in the account to indicate "I was told that" or "it is widely believed that"?

The answer lies in the conventions of eighteenth-century English educated writing. Whether writing a letter to a friend or an official report, writing was a performance. The genteel writer did not show inner feelings, save those of delicacy and kindness. Hesitation and second-guessing in writing were impolite. Indeed, it undermined

6. William Bull to the Board of Trade, October 5, 1739.

the trust that members of the elite were supposed to have for one another's communications. One stated one's case boldly but without boasting. Such writing then conferred on the author an authority that exceeded that of firsthand information or special knowledge. In short, the veracity of the account lay in the person of the writer rather than in the evidence he offered or the sources he used.[7]

There was, in addition, an oral culture of rumor among whites that can be documented; among slaves it must be inferred. The long decade of the 1730s (including 1729 and 1741) was filled with real and imagined slave uprisings throughout the Caribbean and the British mainland colonies. What may be called a "conspiracy panic" grew out of the compounding of these real and rumored rebellions, a kind of aftershock phenomenon one sees following an earthquake. Colonial authorities sent reports back to England, and echoes of these returned in various ways to the colonies. For every written word, there must have been thousands of conversations among whites in colonies with slaves. As the information spread among the colonists, it gained a kind of corporeal shape, ghosts becoming substantial. These, in turn, fueled more rumors. Sometimes the rumors gave impetus to action, as when authorities interpreted a gathering of slaves at the market, or at some domestic celebration, as the beginning of a rebellion or the meeting of conspirators. The result might be nothing more

7. Richard Bushman, *The Refinement of America: Persons, Houses, Cities* (New York: Knopf, 1992), 90–92; Richard D. Brown, *Knowledge Is Power: The Diffusion of Information in Early America* (New York: Oxford University Press, 1989), 52; Sandra M. Gustafson, *Eloquence Is Power: Oratory and Performance in Early America* (Chapel Hill: University of North Carolina Press, 2000), 158.

than the breaking up of the gathering, or it might be a series of summary trials and executions.

One cannot trace with any precision the spread of information among the slave communities. Some scholars, including Mark Smith, Philip Morgan, and John Thornton, are wary of generalizations about long-distance slave conspiracies. Other scholars cite the relative freedom with which slave mariners traveled throughout the Caribbean and along the shore of the North American mainland as potentially supporting communication systems among the slaves. In the Stono rebellion, there is no doubt that the promise of freedom in Spanish Florida motivated men who marched down the Pon Pon on Sunday. Did these men also know of previous rumored and real uprisings in the Caribbean? Slaves found guilty of some part in conspiracies might find themselves sold from one colony to another. Did they carry with them the information of real conspiracies? Surely some did. But we cannot know for certain. We know only that white authorities thought that slaves transmitted information about rebellion and joined in conspiracies based on this information.[8]

But the problem with such rumors, even when based on overheard conversations among slaves about some plot or other, was that slaves were always talking about some plot or other. The talk was a crime in itself (conspiracy), but there might be nothing at all to the talk, as authorities sometimes later admitted and

8. See Charles R. Foy, "Ports of Slavery, Ports of Freedom: How Slaves Used Northern Seaports' Maritime Industry to Escape and Create TransAtlantic Identities—1713–1783," PhD diss., Rutgers University, 2008; and David Barry Gaspar, *Bondsmen and Rebels* (Baltimore: Johns Hopkins University Press, 1985).

slave owners knew all too well. Discontented and malcontented slaves—in other words, just about every slave at some time during the day—would mutter dire threats and fantasize great risings to another. Slaves who were unfairly treated by an overseer or master would return to the quarters and think aloud about what they would do, if they could do it. Another slave reporting that he or she overheard such talk might be rewarded with clothing, money, or even freedom—an inducement to elaborate and extemporize on what was actually said.[9]

Historians have labored mightily to draw meaning from these primary sources. As Peter Wood wrote in the first modern account of the uprising, "I have bypassed derivative second sources and pieced together the following description of the Stono Uprising from the contemporary materials which survive." In the gaps and inconsistencies in the original accounts one can also infer important pieces of information. As Wood was quick to note, most important are the missing voices of the slaves. The entire story is told by whites, some of them far distant from the actual events. This allowed rumor and fear to intervene and exaggerate. But are "precise motives and reasoning" of the slaves involved "beyond historical inquiry"? What about the aims of the whites?[10]

9. See Jason Sharples, "'Something Which This Deponent Did Not Articulately Hear': Oblique Information, Acute Fear, and the Domestic Menace of Slave Conspiracy," paper read to the McNeil Center for Early American Studies, Philadelphia, January 15, 2010.

10. Peter Wood, *Black Majority: Negroes in Colonial South Carolina through the Stono Rebellion* (New York: Norton, 1973), 315n26; Robert Olwell, *Masters, Slaves, and Subjects: The Culture of Power in the South Carolina Low Country, 1740–1790* (Baltimore: Johns Hopkins University Press, 1998), 21.

We are left with mysteries within mysteries. Like the criminalists on the television program *CSI*, we have the bodies and must piece together the evidence to arrive at the most plausible reconstruction of what happened. Even if we can never know for certain what happened on September 8 and 9, 1739, the evidence must nevertheless be weighed in light of a set of rules. These come from hundreds of years of historical scholarship, passed down through generations of teachers to students.

As to style, I follow the lead of the legal scholar Lea VanderVelde, in her imaginative and convincing biography of Harriett Scott, the wife of Dred Scott: "I have not been content to report the evidence with the ubiquitous 'may.' Many things may have happened, and if the possibility is that slight, I neglected to speculate on possibilities that seemed improbable....We have no alternative but to speculate on these lives using the best means possible. Otherwise, we leave them unimagined and thereby risk, as a result of the silence inflicted upon them, creating the false impression that only the lettered contributed to history."[11]

To fill the void that the scarcity of historical documents leaves, I have borrowed approaches from other intellectual and literary disciplines, methods that social scientists and writers have developed to deal with their subjects when there are gaps in the record or the record is silent. The first method is "bricolage," borrowed from anthropology. When Claude Levi-Strauss tried to reconstruct the mythological thinking of "the savage mind," he posited

11. Lea VanderVelde, *Mrs. Dred Scott: A Life on Slavery's Frontier* (New York: Oxford University Press, 2009), 5.

that the primitive thinker was a "bricoleur," one who "makes do with whatever is at hand." The materials and methods available to him are limited, but he constructs from the closed set of things and skills a working model.[12]

Applying the practice of bricolage, we bring to the Stono story documents not obviously related to it—land surveys, lease records, legislative debates, and statute books—that help frame the story. Think of a portrait whose central figure is missing. By painting all the surrounding figures, one can better see the outlines of the central figure. Legal records tell us who lived where and what they wanted out of life.

A second social science technique, comparative vertical or cross-sectional analysis, brings insights and findings from distant places to bear on our subject. Comparative studies of slavery have yielded important insights, revealing differences in addition to similarities. The most important of these comparisons reveals a unique feature of slavery in the British Empire. Within the slave regimes of the Dutch, Spanish, Portuguese, and French colonies in the Americas, the disfiguring lines of racism were not as strictly drawn as in the British colonies. Large communities of freed slaves and mixed-race slaves appeared in Mexico, the Spanish Caribbean, Dutch Guiana, and Portuguese Brazil. In the British sugar islands of Jamaica and Barbados, and in the North American mainland colonies, however, dark skin implied slave status, and, for most Africans, that status was permanent.

---

12. Claude Levi-Strauss, *The Savage Mind*, trans. Doreen and John Weightman (Chicago: University of Chicago Press, 1966), 17.

There are problems in this kind of vertical comparison. David Brion Davis, perhaps the foremost student of comparative slavery, warns that "the history of slavery is an immense and complex subject," adding that "because of the number of variables, the conflicting and inadequate evidence, and the lack of rigorous comparative studies, we simply do not know enough to make precise comparisons or universally valid generalizations." Nevertheless, Davis's own remarkable comparative studies, along with the pioneering comparisons of slavery in the United States with slavery in Brazil, and the more recent studies by Ira Berlin and Philip Morgan, do reveal aspects of Stono otherwise hidden. So, for example, we borrow materials from Caribbean and African slave rebellions to throw light on Stono. Similarly, we utilize accounts of plantation life from other colonies to make sense of life in the Low Country slave quarters.[13]

Finally, to fill gaps in missing records, some historians have resorted to the inspiration of the historical novel. Ordinarily, the author of historical fiction relies on historical scholarship for detail and context. We can reverse that relationship, however. In a 1998 essay for the *American Historical Review*, the historian John Demos reported that he learned the "strategies,

13. David Brion Davis, *The Problem of Slavery in Western Culture* (New York: Oxford University Press, 1988), 30, 53. See also Ira Berlin, *Many Thousands Gone: The First Two Centuries of Slavery in North America* (Cambridge, Mass.: Harvard University Press, 1998); Ira Berlin and Philip D. Morgan, eds., *Slaves' Economy: Independent Production by Slaves in the Americas* (London: Cass, 1991); and the pioneering study—Frank Tannenbaum, *Slave and Citizen: The Negro in the Americas* (New York: Knopf, 1947).

the techniques, the 'moves'" to re-create a full-bodied past from fragments that survived from reading historical novels. Adapting the literary skills of the novelist enables the historian to peer over, if not cross, the "boundary" between fact-based scholarship and fiction. The trick, according to Demos, was to combine an almost excessive concern with those details that could be verified with a common sense of the human condition, the very ties that bound us to people in the past. Thus, Jane Kamensky, in her novelesque re-creation of the life and times of the financial speculator Andrew Dexter in the first decades of the nineteenth century, bids her reader, "Imagine yourself a man on the make, son of a New England farmer from an enlightened village." Thus begins a tale reminiscent of Charles Dickens's *Great Expectations*, as "you dream of trading the plow and the field for the pen and the ledger" to become a "paper man" like Dexter.[14]

Adapting novelistic techniques to fill in gaps is especially useful when historians want to write the lives of ordinary people. Most folks do not leave much of a paper trail. In the past, when literacy was hardly universal and writing took time, effort, and the money to pay for paper, pen, and ink, ordinary people simply passed from view without a documented record of their lives other than birth,

14. John P. Demos, "In Search of Reasons for Historians to Read Novels," *American Historical Review* 103 (December 1998), 1527; Jane Kamensky, *The Exchange Artist: A Tale of High-Flying Speculation and America's First Banking Collapse* (New York: Viking, 2007), 176. The best-known example of this novelesque technique is Demos's own *Unredeemed Captive: A Family Story from Early America* (New York: Knopf, 1994).

marriage, and death. This included most slaves, particularly in the eighteenth century. Novelesque techniques allow us to think about what might have happened at Hutchenson's store that night, what the slaves were thinking in the field alongside Pon Pon Road, and how masters coped with the memory of Stono.

Like the novelist, I walked the land at the time of the year that the events occurred. The air, the water, and the coastline are not precisely the same, but the heat and the humidity, the sensory quality of darkness, give a sense of a place long ago. This is what is called living history, and its techniques are standard in historical reenactments and living museums such as Colonial Williamsburg and Jamestown Place.

So, throughout the preceding pages, I have openly speculated, engaging in a critical conversation with the primary sources. I have borrowed from the social sciences and compared the evidence across time and place. I have looked for the telling detail, the faint footprint of the past that has survived. If I have been persuasive, it is because creative imagination and expertise came together as I read the evidence. But no historical account is final, because no historical account can be definitive, certainly not one of events so cloaked in mystery as those at Stono.[15]

15. Indeed, Stono remains such a difficult topic for historians that the best of our profession sometimes get it wrong. Then there is the popular or folk version; for example, Michael Coker's *Charleston Curiosities* (Charleston, S.C.: History Press, 2008). The account begins: "Moments ago they were secure. Nearly one hundred of the newly liberated were gathered in this cleared field by the water to sing, dance, sound the drums, and drink." The rebels were never secure, not until they entered Florida, and probably not until they were safely within St. Augustine. Nor were they liberated. Coker has a definitive figure for the original band [of] "twenty slaves." No

source given. He has them assemble "along a sluggish creek known today as Wallace River," from which "they moved to Hutchenson's store" next to the bridge, as we know they did in the late evening. Apparently it took them the entire night to get from the store back to Wallace's tavern, close to their starting point at the confluence of Wallace Creek and the Stono River. Then "muskets primed and shouldered they began their march" as though they were British redcoats. Even the militia knew not to prime the muskets until they were ready to fire them—the powder primer would fall out of the pan. The rest of the account is equally improbable, as is that found on a Prentice Hall (textbook) documentary Web site: "The Stono Rebellion was the largest uprising of enslaved Africans to take place during the colonial period. On the morning of September 9, 1739, about twenty slaves in Saint Pauls' Parish, South Carolina, broke into a small store and took guns, powder, and shot. When the owners of the store suddenly arrived, they were killed and their heads were left on the porch. From here, the slaves, led by Jemmy, tried to make their way to Saint Augustine, where the Spanish government had promised them freedom. On their way, they recruited others to join them, while at the same time killing any whites who crossed their path. That evening, they were overtaken and defeated by the colony's militia." This is the "headnote"—the introductory summary—preceding the Oglethorpe report. But Stono was not the largest slave revolt in the period—that title goes to any of a number of slave uprisings in the Caribbean. There is no evidence that the owners of the store arrived during the break-in or that they were indeed owners of the store—that is dramatic license. Next, the Spanish government had not promised the Stono rebels anything; the proclamation of freedom was a general one. Finally, the battle in the field occurred in late afternoon, not in the evening.

INDEX

INDEX